Richard Long

A Line Made by Walking

Dieter Roelstraete

One Work Series Editor
Mark Lewis

Afterall Books Editorial Directors
Charles Esche and Mark Lewis

Managing Editor
Pablo Lafuente

Associate Editor
Caroline Woodley

Copy Editor
Deirdre O' Dwyer

Picture Editor
Gaia Alessi

Other titles in the *One Work* series:

Bas Jan Ader: In Search of the Miraculous
by Jan Verwoert

Hollis Frampton: (nostalgia)
by Rachel Moore

Ilya Kabakov: The Man Who Flew into Space from his Apartment
by Boris Groys

Richard Prince: Untitled (couple)
by Michael Newman

Joan Jonas: I Want to Live in the Country (And Other Romances)
by Susan Morgan

Mary Heilmann: Save the Last Dance for Me
by Terry R. Myers

Marc Camille Chaimowicz: Celebration? Realife
by Tom Holert

Yvonne Rainer: The Mind is a Muscle
by Catherine Wood

Fischli and Weiss: The Way Things Go
by Jeremy Millar

Andy Warhol: Blow Job
by Peter Gidal

Alighiero e Boetti: Mappa
by Luca Cerizza

Chris Marker: La Jetée
by Janet Harbord

Hanne Darboven: Cultural History 1880–1983
by Dan Adler

Michael Snow: Wavelength
by Elizabeth Legge

Sarah Lucas: Au Naturel
by Amna Malik

Marcel Duchamp: Étant donnés
by Julian Jason Haladyn

One Work is a unique series of books published by Afterall, based at Central Saint Martins College of Art and Design in London. Each book presents a single work of art considered in detail by a single author. The focus of the series is on contemporary art and its aim is to provoke debate about significant moments in art's recent development.

Over the course of more than one hundred books, important works will be presented in a meticulous and generous manner by writers who believe passionately in the originality and significance of the works about which they have chosen to write. Each book contains a comprehensive and detailed formal description of the work, followed by a critical mapping of the aesthetic and cultural context in which it was made and has gone on to shape. The changing presentation and reception of the work throughout its existence is also discussed, and each writer stakes a claim on the influence 'their' work has on the making and understanding of other works of art.

The books insist that a single contemporary work of art (in all of its different manifestations), through a unique and radical aesthetic articulation or invention, can affect our understanding of art in general. More than that, these books suggest that a single work of art can literally transform, however modestly, the way we look at and understand the world. In this sense the *One Work* series, while by no means exhaustive, will eventually become a veritable library of works of art that have made a difference.

First published in 2010
by Afterall Books

Afterall
Central Saint Martins
College of Art and Design,
University of the Arts London,
107–109 Charing Cross Road,
London WC2H ODU
www.afterall.org

ISBN Paperback: 978–1–84638–058–7
ISBN Cloth: 978–1–84638–060–0

Distribution by The MIT Press,
Cambridge, Massachusetts and London
www.mitpress.mit.edu

Art Direction and Typeface Design
A2/SW/HK

Printed and bound by
Die Keure, Belgium

The *One Work* series is printed
on FSC certified papers

Supported by
ARTS COUNCIL
ENGLAND

Richard Long

A Line Made by Walking

Dieter Roelstraete

I would like to thank Richard Long and Monika Szewczyk. The editors would also like to thank Ben Tufnell at Haunch of Venison for his assistance with providing images to illustrate this publication.

Dieter Roelstraete is a curator at MuHKA, the Antwerp museum of contemporary art. He is also a tutor at de Appel in Amsterdam and at Piet Zwart Institute in Rotterdam. He is an editor of *Afterall* journal, and has written extensively on contemporary art and related philosophical issues.

Sit as little as possible; credit no thought not born
in the open air and while moving freely about – in which
the muscles too do not hold a festival.
– Friedrich Nietzsche, *Ecce Homo* [1]

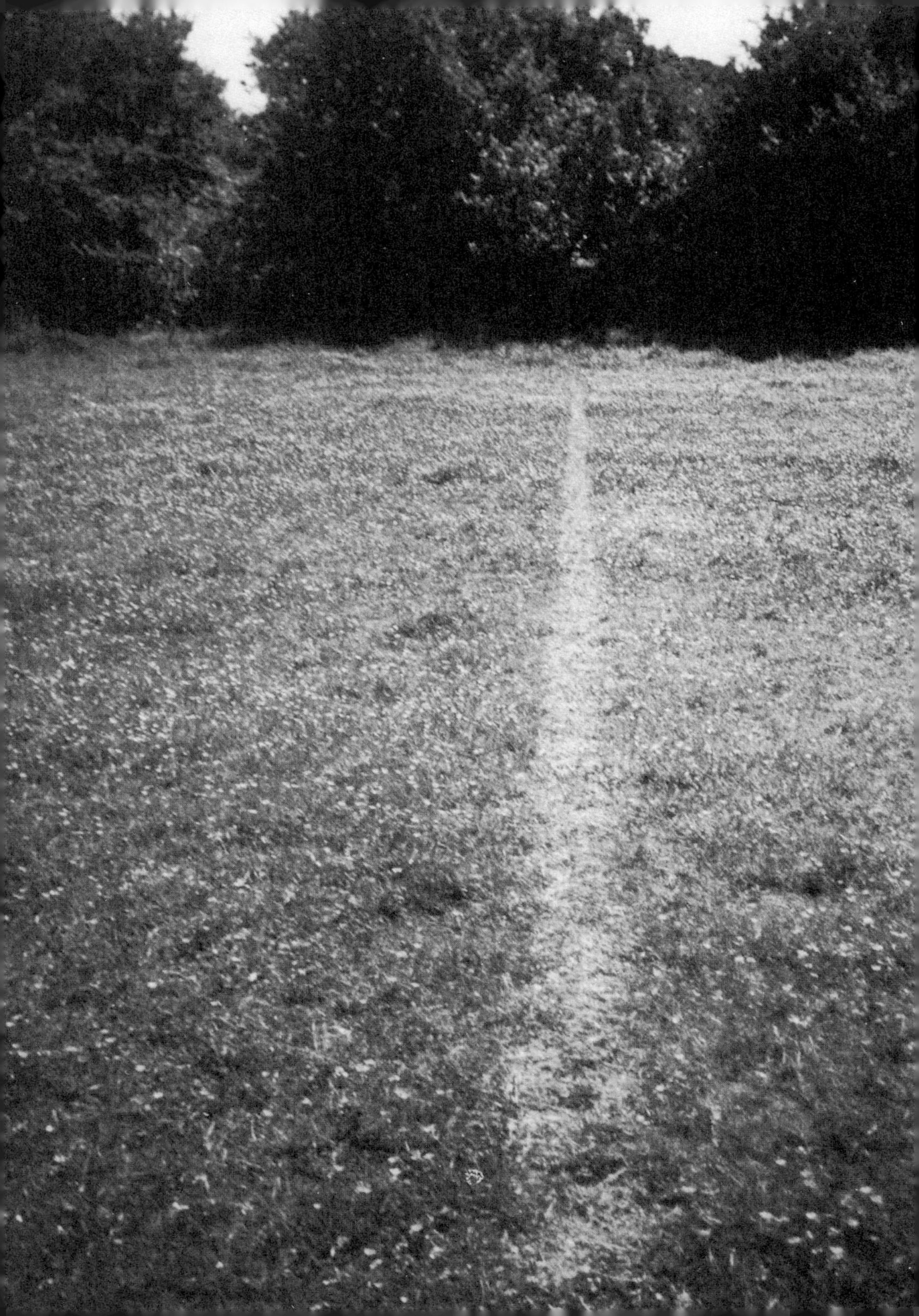

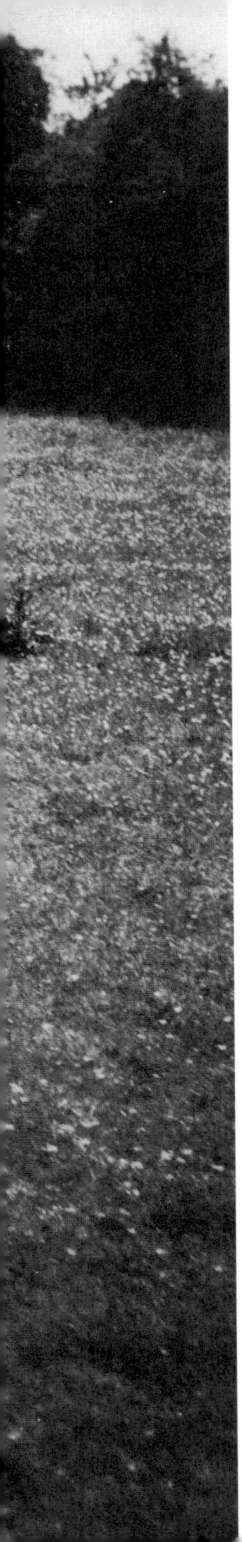

A LINE MADE BY WALKING ENGLAND 1967

cover and previous pages

Richard Long,
A Line Made by Walking, 1967

Ante Scriptum: A Note on Method and Form

Q: Do you ever get lost?
A: There are different ways of getting lost, but never fundamentally lost.
— Richard Long in conversation with Richard Cork[2]

Richard Long's *A Line Made by Walking* (1967; fig.1) may be a straight one, but the telling of its story is anything but a straightforward affair — emphatically *not* a straight story, then. As is well known by anyone who has ever spent a whole day walking — hiking, strolling, traipsing, etc.[3] — the pleasures of such walking are very often contained in straying off the straight and narrow path, in venturing off the beaten track; it is certainly the preferred method for enjoying city life, and getting lost is part of the thrill and charm of every walk's possibilities. This account of Long's work will at times resemble a rhapsodic, meandering ramble rather than the straight line it intently looks back upon, a walk along the crooked path of art.

Veering Off the Beaten Track

I have to report that one fine morning, I do not know any more for sure what time it was, as the desire to take a walk came over me, I put my hat on my head, left my writing room, or room of phantoms, and ran down the stairs to hurry out into the street. [...] *As far as I can remember as I write this down, I found myself, as I walked into the open, bright and cheerful street, in a romantically adventurous state of mind, which pleased me profoundly. The morning world spread out before my eyes appeared as beautiful to me as if I saw it for the first time. Everything I saw made upon me a delightful impression of friendliness, of goodliness and of youth. I quickly forgot that up in my room I had only just a moment before been brooding gloomily over a blank sheet of paper. All sorrow, all pain and all grave thoughts were as vanished, although I vividly sensed a certain seriousness, a tone, still before me and behind me. I was tense with eager expectation*

of whatever might encounter me or cross my way on my walk.
— Robert Walser, 'The Walk'[4]

All kinds and types of dematerialisation, disappearance and evaporation were definitely in the air in the summer of 1967 when Richard Long, then a 22-year-old student at St. Martin's School of Art in London, 'made' the work of art that more or less sealed and secured his inclusion in most canonical historiographies of early Conceptual, Environmental and performance art, *A Line Made by Walking*.

The work is essentially known as a straightforward black-and-white photograph of a line of flattened, trampled-upon grass made by repetitively walking up and down an unidentified field in the countryside just outside London, which we may presume regained its natural upright position soon after Long had left, with only a photograph as lasting evidence of his 'action'. It is also a groundbreaking, early example of a critical movement in art towards the final dismantling of one of the last remaining myths of the post-Duchampian avant-garde: that the work should indeed be 'made' or produced *at all* — that an object should emerge at the tail end of the (linear!) process of artistic production.[5]

Informed, in no small part, by the then-dominant plastic idiom of North American Minimalism,[6] *A Line Made by Walking* equally belongs to the histories of early Conceptual art, Land art (not a label which Long ever felt very comfortable with), performance or body art, Arte Povera (which, incidentally, was also given its definitive name in 1967)[7] and conceptually inflected experimentation in photography. Above all, however, *A Line Made by Walking* most emphatically embodies the basic tenets of a certain 'ism' no longer in use today, simply because it has proven to be so influential that almost all art made since its unassuming beginnings in the mid to late 1960s has come to be seen as essentially derived from it or resistant to it. This 'ism' was 'non-object art', an art of powerful ideas ('idea art' was another early contender for naming this intangible 'ism') encoded in fleeting gestures and ethereal interventions — some, though by no means all, documented either photographically or in writing — that obstinately, programmatically refused and resisted all attempts to reduce art to the mere production of art objects. This loose grouping of movements and tendencies sought to bring art closer to the everyday by radically re-imagining the old dream of dissolving art into life, rejecting the twinned concepts of skill and economic value and tearing down the walls of both the studio and the exhibition space as the traditional validating institutions of art-making and viewing. It appeared bound up in part with the (largely youth-driven) cultural phenomenon of political protest then just gaining critical momentum around the globe, aimed in no small measure against the consumerist, commodity-obsessed 'society of the spectacle' of the 1960s. Finally, and this is especially true of emblematic works such as *A Line Made by Walking*, it was instrumental in establishing an ethic and aesthetic of productive, fruitful confusion as one of the dominant paradigms of post-1960s art — the revolutionary blurring of disciplinary boundaries between methods and forms, on the one hand, and form and content, on the other. This blurring is best expressed in one of the most urgent questions triggered by the encounter of a contemporary viewer with a work such as Long's *A Line Made by Walking*: is (was) the art in the *walking*, in the *line* made by walking, or in the *photograph* made of the line made by walking? Did the work exist for no longer than the twenty minutes it took Long to make the narrow strip of flattened grass appear, or does the work continue to exist in its ongoing transportation, as one of the more potent rumours within Conceptual art folklore, across time, all the way up to its current, book-length consideration? Are we currently in the process of remaking *A Line Made by Walking*?[8]

Background

Questioning the artwork

In North American art critic Lucy Lippard's epochal study of early Conceptual art, *Six Years: The Dematerialization of the Art Object from 1966 to 1972* (1973), Long's work appears flanked by, among others, Ed Ruscha's *Thirtyfour Parking Lots* (1967); Dan Graham's 'The Book as Object' (1967); Joseph Kosuth's *Titled (Art as Idea as Idea)* (1967); and the opening, on 2 January 1967, of the Salon de la Jeune Peinture in Paris, which featured the landmark exhibition by BMPT (Daniel Buren, Olivier Mosset, Michel Parmentier and Niele Toroni) — an exhibition of paintings made by artists who no longer considered themselves to be painters and who consequently withdrew from the Salon a day after its opening. Throughout this period, the artworks themselves became less and less tangible, the 'rules' of their production appearing more and more arbitrary, irrevocably dissolving in a riot of 'actions' in a process shaped in no small part by a heightened dependence on processes of mechanical reproduction.

Certainly, the pioneers of early Conceptual art listed above were by no means the first to explore the critical possibilities of the 'dematerialisation of the art object' as a way out of various (artistic *and* political) cul-de-sacs facing artists around the globe in the wake, most poignantly, of the devastation of World War II — a devastation that modernist high culture, with all its precious objects, its high production values and adoration of artistic prowess, had been so conspicuously powerless to stop from happening. In what could be read as a response to the famous Adornian quip that writing poetry after Auschwitz effectively constitutes an act of barbarity, many artists explored the possibility of erasing 'writing' (or other types of art production) altogether, with this erasure itself constituting an act of writing.[9] Taking up the legacy of Dada — itself partly the product of a previous World War — Yves Klein had created *Le Vide* (*The Void*, 1958) and 'leapt into the void' (1960), and Piero

Manzoni canned his own (artist's) excrement (*Merda d'artista*, or *Artist's Shit*, 1961) and signed living people's bodies (*Scultura vivente*, or *Living Sculpture*, 1961). In a similar vein, in 1953 Robert Rauschenberg had erased a Willem de Kooning drawing, and titled it, matter-of-factly, *Erased de Kooning Drawing*. Also in a short period between 1954 and 1956, a group of artists in Japan had assembled under the banner of Gutai to make art with painted hens, rain and footsteps.[10] The most sustained contribution to the expanding field of immaterial art, however, came in the shape of the Fluxus revolution that washed over Europe in the early 1960s, and the various happenings that were staged in the United States at around the same time. Blending the formidable visionary talents of Joseph Beuys, John Cage, Allan Kaprow and George Maciunas, these 'movements', though lacking the militancy and knack for radicalism typical of much early Conceptual art, effectively helped to clear the path which Richard Long was very soon to tread himself, towing away the debris left behind by staid and discredited past art movements to reveal a blank slate ready to receive the outrageous (and outrageously simple) idea that walking could be art, and that a line made by walking could be an artwork.

The Linesman

Born in Bristol just after the end of World War II, Long grew up in a Britain marked by scarcity, by a certain 'austerity' even.[11] He has often cited the entwinement of two particular childhood experiences as the defining, formative influence on his early career in art, and in the field of Land art specifically: his being seen as the burgeoning artist in his family and his spending most of his free time rambling in the countryside. His grandparents, whom he visited often as a child, lived in the countryside (near Dartmoor, Devon), and his parents were walking enthusiasts who spent most of their family holidays in the West Country. Long lives in the countryside outside Bristol to this day, and has always identified himself as a 'rural' artist, which is not as conventional or unproblematic a claim as it may seem.[12] Walking as a sport or recreational activity can, of course, pride itself on a formidable history, but in post-War Britain it acquired a novel, subtly politicised dimension, prompting Marxist historian Raphael Samuel to single out 'hiking as a major, if unofficial, component of the socialist lifestyle'.[13] It was also deeply embedded in an idealist ethos of militant amateurism, which was, in the 1960s, being tapped into by aspiring young artists around the globe. Long has continued to espouse the ideal of the amateur — 'doing it for the love of it' — to this day. Long the 'family artist', then, developed a voracious appetite for artistic stimuli early in life, and started making his first sculptures in his parents' garden sometime in the early 1960s.

Another early revelatory aesthetic experience followed a visit to Tate Gallery in London in 1964, when the nineteen-year-old artist caught a first shimmering glimpse of the way ahead for modern sculpture — a Gulbenkian exhibition, titled '1954—1964', included a considerable number of sculptures lying on the floor, without the traditional and tradition-laden sculptural accoutrements of pedestal, plinth and socle. Seeing one particular Isamu Noguchi work not only gave Long his first ideas for the floor sculptures that continue to pop up in his work to the present day (the first sculptures in that vein were made in 1965), but also decisively diverted his attention towards the floor as such — towards the surface of the earth upon which we walk. This would, in time, clearly prove to be an even more significant, transformative insight, literally grounding his subsequent practice in a novel understanding of art.

Long enlisted in the West of England College of Art in Bristol in 1962, but the precocious young artist proved a little too adventurous for his peers and teachers, and was eventually kicked out. In 1966, he decided to continue his studies at London's St. Martin's School of Art, which had just introduced a new programme perfectly suited to the young artist's inquisitive inclinations: an independent sculpture course headed by Anthony Caro and Phillip King that counted a young George Passmore (of later Gilbert & George fame) and Hamish Fulton (the 'other' British walking artist, whom Long would collaborate with on numerous occasions throughout his career) among its student body.[14] Long still remembers making his first sculptures on the roof of the main school building during this period of relatively carefree artistic experimentation in an uncommonly free environment. He often travelled back and forth between Bristol and London, by hitch-hiking or cycling, along the old A4 road before it was supplanted by the M4 motorway (begun in 1961 and only completed in the 1990s). Travelling through a part of southern England marked by the presence of ancient archaeological remains, which he eventually came to know as well as the proverbial back of his hand. The most memorable point of reference would always be Silbury Hill, right next to the A4, a forty-metre-high earthen mound made around 2400 BC, near Avebury in Wiltshire — the largest of its kind in Europe. Avebury lay several miles north of the much more famous Neolithic stone circle at Stonehenge, which Long (who warns against too direct a reading of his sculptural work as somehow responding to England's megalithic culture) got to see at age 21. He does acknowledge, however, an early coincidental interest in the entirely speculative theory of so-called 'ley lines' formulated by English amateur archaeologist Alfred Watkins in *The Old Straight Track: Its Mounds, Beacons, Moats, Sites and Mark Stones* (1925). Essentially a genealogical hypothesis concerning the alignment of certain landscape features across England, Watkins's ley line theory (which Long was first made aware of at his Whitechapel show in 1971) chimes in exemplarily well

A Line Made by Walking | 7

with Long's own formative early interest in the phenomenon of alignment and the basic figure of the line.

In the meantime, Long had begun making a couple of works that presaged *A Line Made by Walking*, the most important perhaps being a snowball track made on the Clifton Downs in 1964 (fig.2) — a prototypical line drawing made by rolling a growing ball of snow over a patch of grass, freeing up its meandering path in the process. This three-dimensional 'drawing' was followed, in 1966, by his first earth work, *Turf Circle*, a negative shape cut out of the ground in the Longs' neighbours' garden.

All these scattered forces and interests fortuitously coalesced in 1967 when, one day in June, Long got on a train at Waterloo Station and rode southwest, into the countryside. A mere twenty miles outside the city centre, Long decided to get off (he now no longer remembers the exact location), walked up to a featureless field of grass he had just seen from the train, and proceeded to 'make' a line in it by walking. It took him some twenty minutes to 'walk the line', and by the time he was done enough sunlight had shone down upon it to make it visible (to him as well as to the viewer); as a matter of fact, it was sunlight, more than the amount of times the artist walked up and down the same straight path, that really made it apparent. Here already, an early aleatory, quasi-Cagean element was allowed to creep in and co-determine the work, symbolising the artist's readiness to hand over part of his control over the final outcome of the creative process: Long hadn't planned for the line to be made on an especially sunny day — the sun just happened to be shining, and this in turn made the line appear all the more present, or at least visible enough for the artist's purposes. Having reached the desired effect of a simple straight line in an unidentified field of grass, Long then made the picture which has since been reproduced in innumerable anthologies, history books and monographs — the black-and-white photograph, frontally taken, of a narrow strip of trampled grass thinning out towards the horizon. Incidentally, Long also photographed the line from the side but found the result, in his own words, 'not terribly interesting visually' — an early manifestation of his deviation from Conceptual art orthodoxy, which clamorously, and not always truthfully, denied any interest in the aesthetic quality of an idea's execution. After this short sojourn in the countryside, Long took a train back to London, had his film developed at a local chemist's (only subsequent prints were made by the artist himself) — and the rest, as they say, is history.

Walking, or: Turning Time into Space

At the beginning Richard Long proudly identified himself as a sculptor, and he is perhaps better known today for his driftwood circles and monumental, floor-covering 'lines' of turf, coal or slate than for his ephemeral work from the late 1960s and early 70s (figs.3—4). The line made by walking *is* also a sculpture — a very transient and humble one for sure, but a sculpture nonetheless. As an imprint, a form or shape, a physical fact both 'inside' and added to the landscape, its ambiguity serves as a clear marker of the artist's aspirations to stretch and test the boundaries of the expanding field of sculpture. In this his work obviously relates to the North American movement of Land art, in terms of its aspirations to be recognised as a continuation of a tradition in sculpture broadened by Minimalism, which today strike us as perfectly sensible. Land artists like Walter De Maria, Michael Heizer, Nancy Holt and Robert Smithson made big, immovable things that required a great deal of physical effort and material expertise, just like Michelangelo, Auguste Rodin and Tony Smith. This enthusiasm for grandiose, sweeping gestures — for the frontier spirit of conquest, masculinity and monumentalism — was not shared by the young Long. Instead, his forays into the expanded realm of sculpture nearly

›ximated performance art, although this is a tag that Long has always, vigorously and tellingly, rejected, precisely because of its allusion to a quality of theatricality and expressive subjectivity which the decidedly non-personalist or depersonalised aesthetic of his work seems to contradict. This approximation culminated in a series of virtually immaterial works; among them walks whose only 'trace' was a line drawn on a map (for example, *A Ten Mile Walk, England 1968*, 1968; fig.5), or a list of 21 arrows depicting the changing wind direction as experienced by him during a straight ten-mile northward walk on Dartmoor (*Wind Line*, 1985; fig.6). The walk as a work of art in itself, its line-shaped imprint named 'sculpture'; the walk resembling a readymade even: this powerful idea, too, was first fully articulated in *A Line Made by Walking*, England, 1967.

Well before walking was claimed and (re-)invented as an art form in its own right, the walk itself had already been recognised as an important cultural artefact, and the art of walking had become a staple item in the philosophical diet, in particular, of the Western imagination. Some of our culture's greatest and most influential thinkers were avid walkers who often took great pains to document their walks for posterity in an attempt to 'prove' the walk's salutary effects on their thinking habits. Some of their most momentous insights were actually germinated during long, often solitary, quasi-ritualised walks — many, but by no means all, set against a backdrop of virginal natural splendour prone to prompt reflections on the nature of the sublime. In fact, no history of Land and Environmental art appears to be complete without referencing, however frugally, the philosophical discourse on the sublime as initiated by Edmund Burke and Immanuel Kant.[15] The oldest examples of this tradition of walking as a thinking man's art lead us all the way back to ancient Greek customs initiated by the Sophists, Socrates and the Peripatetics ('Wanderers'), a group of Stoics whose first loyalty was not so much to places or schools, but to the much more mobile category of 'ideas'.[16] In the early Middle Ages, troubadours most articulately embodied this idealist vision of a cultural practice engendered by wandering, and early medieval university life was heavily dependent on the principled nomadism of both its tutors and student body. Not until the appearance of the towering figures of European Enlightenment thought, however, does our conception of the daily practice of philosophy become inextricably linked with a well-nigh formalised walking regime that, crucially, is exercised in solitude. Jean-Jacques Rousseau was the first philosopher to name a philosophical treatise (or rather, corpus of philosophical reflections) after the walks that apparently spawned them; *Reveries of a Solitary Walker*, an early example of walking as a practical philosophy of solitude, was published in 1782, four years after his death. In *The Confessions*, he noted: 'I can only meditate when I am walking. When I stop I cease to think; my mind only works with my legs.'[17] It was the experience of reading *The Confessions*, incidentally, which caused another famous *promeneur*, Immanuel Kant, to slip up on a routine that had become so dependable that until that day the inhabitants of Königsberg (present-day Kaliningrad in Russia) would allegedly set their clocks to the exact time of the philosopher's passage through the streets of the Prussian metropolis.[18] Indeed, as Rebecca Solnit notes in *Wanderlust: A History of Walking* (2001):

the association between walking and philosophising became so widespread that central Europe has places named after it: the celebrated Philosophenweg in Heidelberg where Hegel is said to have walked, the Philosophen-damm in Königsberg that Kant passed on his daily stroll (now replaced by a railway station) and the Philosopher's Way Kierkegaard mentions in Copenhagen. [...] *The young Friedrich Nietzsche declares with superb conventionality:*

'For recreation I turn to three things, and a wonderful recreation they provide! — my Schopenhauer, Schumann's music and, finally, solitary walks.[19]

The case of Kierkegaard is perhaps especially intriguing. According to Solnit, 'in a memory he ascribes to one of his pseudonyms but which is almost certainly his own, he tells of how his father, rather than let him leave the house, would walk back and forth in a room with him, describing the world so vividly that the boy seemed to see all the variety evoked'.[20] Defending his later passion for aimlessly roaming the streets of the Danish capital, Kierkegaard often liked to refer to a story ascribed to the original Cynic, Diogenes of Sinope: apparently, 'when the Eleatics denied motion, Diogenes, as everyone knows, came forward as an opponent. He literally did come forward, because he did not say a word but merely paced back and forth a few times, thereby assuming he had sufficiently refuted them.'[21] And Martin Heidegger, one of the Eleatics' most astute readers, devoted an entire (slim) publication not so much to walking itself but, rather more typically to its site and trajectory — instead, that is to say, to the walking path. *Der Feldweg* (*The Pathway*, 1953) includes photographs of an unspectacular countryside road just outside the village of Messkirch in south-west Germany, where Heidegger was born in 1889 and buried in 1976. This village was the scene of many a rambling philosophical conversation, some of which were compiled in his *Holzwege* (freely translated as *Off the Beaten Track*, 1950).

Considering the walk's propensity to foster deep thought, in particular in the phenomenological, embodied vein of late Heidegger, Solnit discusses walking as 'a state in which the mind, the body and the world are aligned, as though they were three characters finally in conversation together. [...] Walking allows us to be in our bodies and in the world without being made busy by them.'[22] In a phrase that seems particularly apt with respect to describing the work of Richard Long, she adds: 'walking is a mode of making the world as well as being in it'.[23] As one of the most ancient modes of humans being *in* the world, it is also the oldest mode of transporting oneself *through* the world — of both measuring the world and appropriating it, of staking out one's territory within it. Indeed, in his celebrated *Practice of Everyday Life* (1980), Michel de Certeau writes that 'the act of walking [...] is a process of appropriation of the topographical system on the part of the pedestrian; it is a spatial acting-out of the place. [...] It implies relations among differentiated positions.' In fact, de Certeau even compares walking to talking — 'the act of walking is to the urban system what the speech act is to language' — making walking into something akin to a 'space of enunciation'.[24] Already here, de Certeau's conceptualisation of walking as somehow integral to the urban fabric brings into play the rural/urban dialectic that is so central to certain strands within the Land art movement, and to Richard Long's practice in particular. And finally, in strictly evolutionary terms, walking (upright) simply came first: it is, in essence, what defines becoming hominid.

In the most rewarding chapter of her history of walking, Solnit locates Long's compatriot, the English Romantic poet William Wordsworth, rather than his philosophising contemporaries, at the origin of a long historical process that culminated in the establishment of walking as a self-conscious cultural act and definite part of aesthetic experience with definite political implications. Before Wordsworth's advent and defiant appropriation of walking as a thinking man's way of life and of making art, the following words, uttered by a German minister named Karl Philipp Moritz while visiting Wordsworth's England, mostly rung true: 'a traveller on foot in this country seems to be considered as a sort of wild man, or an out-of-the-way-being, who is stared at, pitied, suspected and shunned by everybody that meets him'.[25] In fact, walking along the public roads in England often signified that one was either a pauper or a footpad, at least until the 1770s, when various intellectuals and eccentrics began to walk for pleasure. The precise timing is not without significance: the discovery of walking as an aesthetic pleasure pursued for its own 'disinterested' sake unwittingly inaugurated a decade of socio-political change which reached its apogee in the American Revolution of 1776 and the French Revolution of 1789. Indeed, let us be reminded here that the very formula of the aesthetic was only coined a few years earlier, by German philosopher Alexander Baumgarten, to describe what Terry Eagleton has called 'a discourse of the body':

Aesthetics is born as a discourse of the body. In its original formulation by the German philosopher Alexander Baumgarten, the term refers not in the first place to art, but, as the Greek aisthesis would suggest, to the whole region of human perception and sensation, in contrast to the more rarefied domain of conceptual thought. [...] *It is thus the first stirrings of a primitive materialism — of the body's long inarticulate rebellion against the tyranny of the theoretical.* [26]

It is particularly illuminating to read these opening sentences from Eagleton's *The Ideology of the Aesthetic* (1990) in light of the much later art-historical polemic surrounding the puritanical injunctions of some Conceptual art, and the protest this triggered in the shape of much subsequent 'body' and performance art; Richard Long's practice, with its subtle emphasis on the materiality of the earth encountered by the artist's mobile body, certainly belongs to this recent history of rivalling ideas, just as much as it belongs to a larger history of contestation and dissidence with more clearly discernible political aspirations.

Rebecca Solnit further expands on the trinity of radical politics, love of nature and pedestrianism, noting that at this point in time (we are back in the late 1700s) 'travelling any distance on foot was the act of a political radical in England, expressing an unconventionality and a willingness to identify and be identified with the poor' — an early premonition of the politicisation of pedestrianism in post-War Britain echoed by Raphael Samuel. This historical shift in the politics and class allegiance of walking had been prepared, in part, in the transformation of landscaping traditions that unfolded throughout much of the eighteenth century — a revolution in horticulture and gardening *as* landscape painting (to paraphrase Alexander Pope's famous quote) that essentially revolved around the opposition of French versus English landscaping styles. According to this scheme, the English landscape garden as a space for walking was equated with a typically English idea of liberty at first merely distinct from but ultimately opposed to the authoritarian, disciplinary centralism and planning ethos deemed typical of French (political) culture in general, both before and after 1789. Needless to say, this was a conception of *individual* liberty first and foremost; private experience and the various informal art forms associated with this emerging culture of privacy were blooming elsewhere as well, notably in the rise of the novel. In England, towards the end of the Baroque, privately owned gardens were gradually becoming parks, and all kinds of enclosures were slowly disappearing, blending into the surrounding landscape instead. This in turn enabled a radically different, more democratic experience of landscape: 'the middle class was acquiring the hitherto aristocratic taste for landscape. A landscape garden was a luxury that only a few could create or use, but the unaltered landscape was available to virtually everyone, and more and more middle class people could travel to enjoy it as the roads became safer and smoother and transportation became cheaper.'[27] Indeed, towards the end of the eighteenth century, thanks to these various revolutions in transportation, the very nature of travel forever changed:

before the mid-eighteenth century, travel accounts have little to say about the land between religious or cultural landmarks. [...] In pilgrimage and practical travel, the space between home and destination had been an inconvenience or an ordeal. When this space became scenery, travel became an end in itself, an expansion of the garden stroll. That is to say, the experiences along the way could replace destinations as the purpose of travel. And if the whole landscape was the destination, one arrived as soon as one set out in this world that could be looked at as a garden or a painting. Walking had long been recreational, but travel had joined it, and it was only a matter of time before travelling on foot would itself become a widespread part of the pleasures of scenic travel, its slowness finally a virtue.[28]

The Nomadic Art Machine

Much of what we have discussed so far not only concerned walking, but also travel more generally; the 'invention' of walking as a recreational practice in its own right is indeed historically linked to the emergence of a more 'democratic' tourist experience in eighteenth-century Europe, and the walking art of Hamish Fulton and Richard Long is as much related to the hallowed English tradition of country walking as it is to the momentous transformation undergone by the tourist and travel industries in the post-War Western world, and in the early to mid 1960s more specifically. Practicing his art in locales as far-flung as Kilimanjaro (1969), the Andes (1972), the Canadian Prairies (1974), the Himalayas (1975) and Alaska (1977), at a time when these were not yet obvious destinations for an artist still in his late twenties or early thirties, Long's trajectory has come to embody one of the defining features of the contemporary art scene — its mobility, its cultivation of a certain idea of rootlessness and its defiant identification with the figure of the vagrant, the nomad and the exile, all of which would have been unthinkable without the revolutionary democratisation of air travel (among other things) during those decades (figs.7—12). Conceptual art in particular, partly because of its liberating emphasis on the primacy of immaterial ideas over their cumbersome execution, partly because of its political penchant towards a rhetoric of internationalism, contributed in no small measure to these early stirrings of what only much later became known as 'globalisation'. The very idea of the network on which Conceptual art so openly rested necessitated both extensive travel and the invention of new strategies of art-making, such as Mail art or the upgrading of the printed page to fully-fledged 'exhibition' status.[29] The conflation, finally, of Land art and a new type of art tourism (presaging the biennial-driven global tourism of the current art scene) has been amply chronicled: massive Land art projects such as Walter De Maria's *Lightning Field* (1977), Michael Heizer's *Double Negative* (1969—70) and Robert Smithson's *Spiral Jetty* (1970) were not only dependent on the generosity and managerial acumen of adventurous private patrons for their conception and execution, their survival as modern American myths also came to depend in part on the possibility of (relatively) cheap air travel to their remote sites.

The idea of travel as an art form in itself, or at least of travel as an authentic site of aesthetic experience that complicated the post-War triumph of the expanded idea of art, was famously recounted by sculptor Tony Smith in an interview with Samuel Wagstaff in 1966:

When I was teaching at Cooper Union in the first year or two of the 1950s, someone told me how I could get on to the unfinished New Jersey Turnpike. I took three students and drove from somewhere in the Meadows to New Brunswick. It was a dark night and there were no lights or shoulder markers, lines, railings or anything at all except the dark pavement moving through the landscape of the flats, rimmed by hills in the distance, but punctuated by stacks, towers, fumes and coloured lights. This drive was a revealing experience. The road and much of the landscape was artificial, and yet it couldn't be called a work of art. On the other hand, it did something for me that art had never done. At first I didn't know what it was, but its effect was to liberate me from many of the views I had had about art. It seemed that there had been a reality there which had not had any expression in art. [...] *The experience on the road was something mapped out but not socially recognised. I thought to myself, it ought to be clear that's the end of art. Most paintings look pretty pictorial after that. There is no way you can frame it, you just have to experience it.*[30]

The shadow of Jack Kerouac's paean to the motorised odyssey, *On the Road* (1957), still looms large in this fragment, and Smith's monumental shadow would in turn loom large in much subsequent North American Land art. In Long's very different take on Land art, *experiencing* the landscape, rather than rivalling its monumental scale or altering it, would become an overarching concern, and his work has always been, as a rule, more mobile and unstable than that of his North American counterparts. In this sense, too, it is much closer in spirit to contemporary art's defining romance of the nomad, its cultivation of vagrancy and subsequent cult of the rhizome and 'nomadology': the sheer lightness (both literally and metaphorically) and principled mobility of Long's practice, his attachment to an art that can be made anywhere, is perfectly attuned to the reticular paradigm of contemporary art, by which the choice (or ability) to live out of one's suitcase has become a virtue rather than a handicap.[31] Surely today's art world has become entirely unthinkable without cheap, no-frills air travel, prompting many artists to either reflect upon this new-found state of willed rootlessness in their own work or at least dramatically expand the radius of their investigative activities to include the tourist experience as such. Many present-day art-walking projects, such as Joachim Koester's *Kant Walks* (2005) — a suite of photographs depicting the empty streets of Kaliningrad, where two centuries before, Immanuel Kant walked — attest to this fact, as do art practices that effectively appropriate or parody certain tourist tropes, such as the guided tour or guidebook. See, for instance, the work of Los Angeles-based artists collective Center for Land Use Interpretation, which, among other activities, organises bus trips into the Mojave desert in Southern California that include visits to borate mines and aeroplane boneyards; Francis Alÿs's *Seven Walks* (2005) project in London; Janet Cardiff's audio walks in cities such as London, Florence, Pittsburgh, San Francisco and St. Louis, which she began making in the early 1990s (figs.13—14); or Suchan Kinoshita's contribution to the exhibition 'The Celibate's Suitcase' in Maastricht in 1995, which invited visitors to sign up for a 24-hour trip around town in the company of the artist — mostly continuations of the fully-formed tradition of walking as a (performative) art practice.[32]

This long and complex history probably helps to explain why walking was taken up with such fervour by a number of artists in the mid to late 1960s as an effective way to challenge certain sclerotic, literally static preconceptions concerning art, art-making and its institutions — with varying purposes and very different effects. This resulted in a modestly sized but powerful body of pedestrian art practices that in the main appear quietly detached from Richard Long's momentous discovery, in 1967, of walking as a way of making art. The most notable instance is to be found in the work of Dutch Conceptualist Stanley Brouwn, who as early as 1960 started his series *This Way*

Brouwn (1960—64; fig.15), for which he would ask passers-by to sketch the way from point A to B on a piece of paper, which he would then stamp and appropriate as a work. Crucially, Brouwn's early forays into psychogeography were of a more jovial nature than much of the work produced by his contemporaries, while the decidedly urban (i.e. social) dimension of his practice set him apart from the later work of Long and Fulton. Another important point of reference is the 'walking' (if we can really call it that) pioneered by Bruce Nauman in his studio from 1967 to 1968, when he made, out of a well-documented sense of abysmal boredom, the following video performances: *Walking in an Exaggerated Manner Around the Perimeter of a Square*, *Slow Angle Walk (Beckett Walk)*, *Walking with Contrapposto* and *Playing a Note on the Violin While I Walk Around the Studio*. Nauman's interest in obsessive repetition (which he shared with Long) and behavioural constraints would eventually result in his corridor pieces of the early 1970s, prompted by an exploration of the dark side of walking, which also inspired Vito Acconci's *Following Piece* from 1969 (figs.16—17), a performance work for which Acconci chose to follow a random, anonymous person in the crowd around town until this became physically impossible (mostly because the person in question would at some point enter a private space, inevitably turning the work into a reflection upon the embattled dialectic of public and private in the postmodern city). Some years later, French artist Sophie Calle would reverse the roles set out in Acconci's piece and, for *Detective* (1980), hire a private detective to follow *her* around town and make photographs of his subject. Nauman's corridor pieces, Acconci's *Following Piece* and Calle's *Detective* are all rather lugubrious variations on the art of walking that clearly reflect the dystopian urban experience, none of which is discernible in Long's decidedly ahistorical, rambling eulogies to either sublime or humdrum natural beauty.[33] Acconci's work is an especially forceful allusion, furthermore, to the anxiety that surrounds the relationship of the individual to the depersonalised crowds, mobs and multitudes of modern urban culture. His and other artists' walking projects were set in cities rather than deserts, forests, heaths or mountain ranges, and the defining tension here is clearly between the anonymous artist and the subject of his (again, very rarely her) gloating, voyeuristic gaze — the Baudelairean *flâneur* versus the crowd, the freedom-loving creative individual, often driven by transgressive curiosities, versus the impersonal web of reified social relations. Here — upon mentioning the very notion of *flânerie* — it is worth considering Long's work in relation to the history of the Situationist International, which likewise reached a critical juncture in 1967, the year that saw the publication of the movement's most formidable intellectual feat, Guy Debord's *La Société du spectacle* (*The Society of the Spectacle*), which sealed the movement's gradual alienation from the avant-garde art circles from which it had arisen a decade or so earlier. An ironic reversal, then, of the attempts made by Long and other artists at the time to walk *towards* art rather than — in typically contrarian Situationist fashion — *away* from it.

The Situationist International's singular contribution to the historiography of walking as an artistic practice or cultural artefact is concentrated in Debord's well-known 'theory of the *dérive*', or drift-like locomotion without a goal, dating from the late 1950s. According to Debord, 'one of the basic Situationist practices is the *dérive*, a technique of rapid passage through varied ambiances. *Dérives* involve playful-constructive behaviour and awareness of psychogeographical effects, and are thus quite different from the classic notions of journey or stroll.'[34] This is all very fine as far as it goes, but, more pointedly and problematically, even though Debord grudgingly admits than one can in fact practise *dérive* alone:

all indications are that the most fruitful numerical arrangement consists of several small groups of two or three people who have reached the same level of awareness, since cross-checking these different groups' impressions makes it possible to arrive at more objective conclusions. It is preferable for the composition of these groups to change from one dérive *to another. With more than four or five participants, the specifically* dérive *character rapidly diminishes, and in any case it is impossible for there to be more than ten or twelve people without the* dérive *fragmenting into several simultaneous* dérives.[35]

Not only was this nothing like the language in which Richard Long would eventually go on to couch his own brand of drifting, it also set the *dérive* apart from walking as an art form in its crude insistence that the former be a group entertainment (though quite distinct from the 'socialist' rambling of early post-War Britain) — an entertainment, that is, for groups led by Debord. All in all rather odd for a movement (the Situationist International) that appears to descend directly from the foundational cultivation of solitude in the critical writings of modernity's original bard, Charles Baudelaire, whose exemplary *flânerie* prompted Walter Benjamin to venture that 'the idleness of the *flâneur* is a demonstration against the division of labour', and that 'basic to *flânerie* is the idea that the fruits of idleness are more precious than the fruits of labour'.[36] This quote highlights the crucial, defining difference between Long's work and the labour-intensive Land art projects of his North American counterparts, whose toilsome work so often required whole battalions of dump trucks and huge digging machines; it also seems an apt description of the basic emptiness and picture of *absence* that haunt Long's *A Line Made by Walking* — a line, we might say, made by deliberate idling. In essence, this was an early hunch of the walker's fundamental alignment with the *vita contemplativa* of the artist as *non-producer*. In fact,

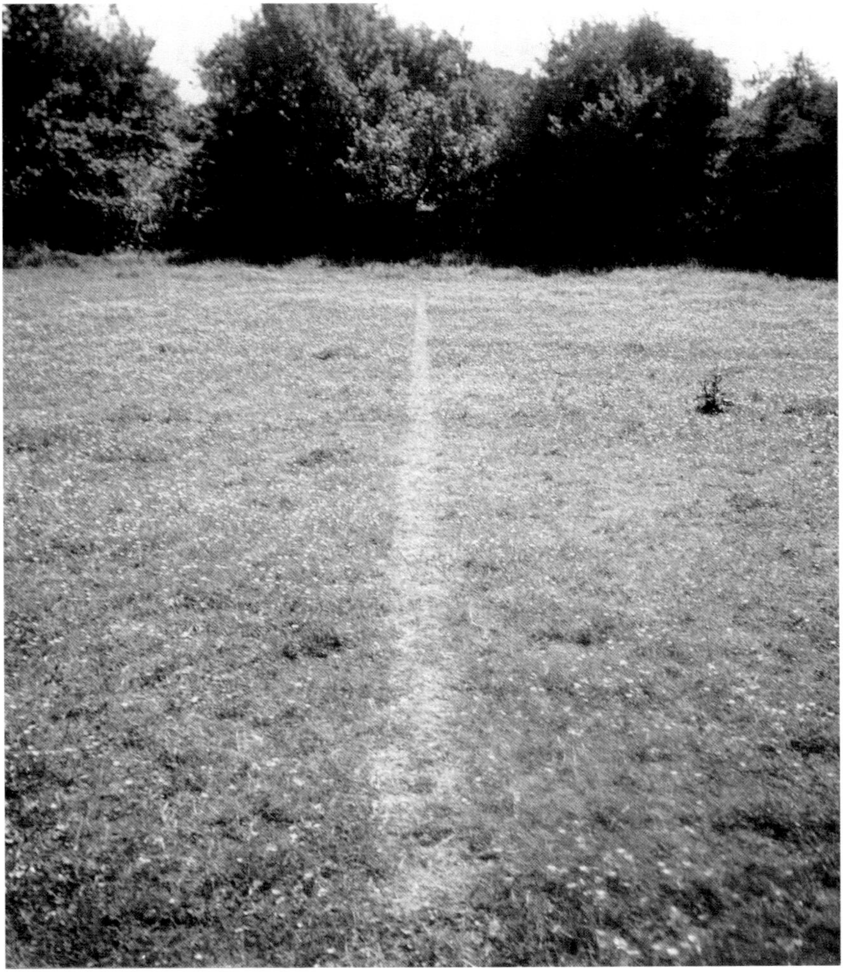

1. Richard Long,
A Line Made by Walking, 1967

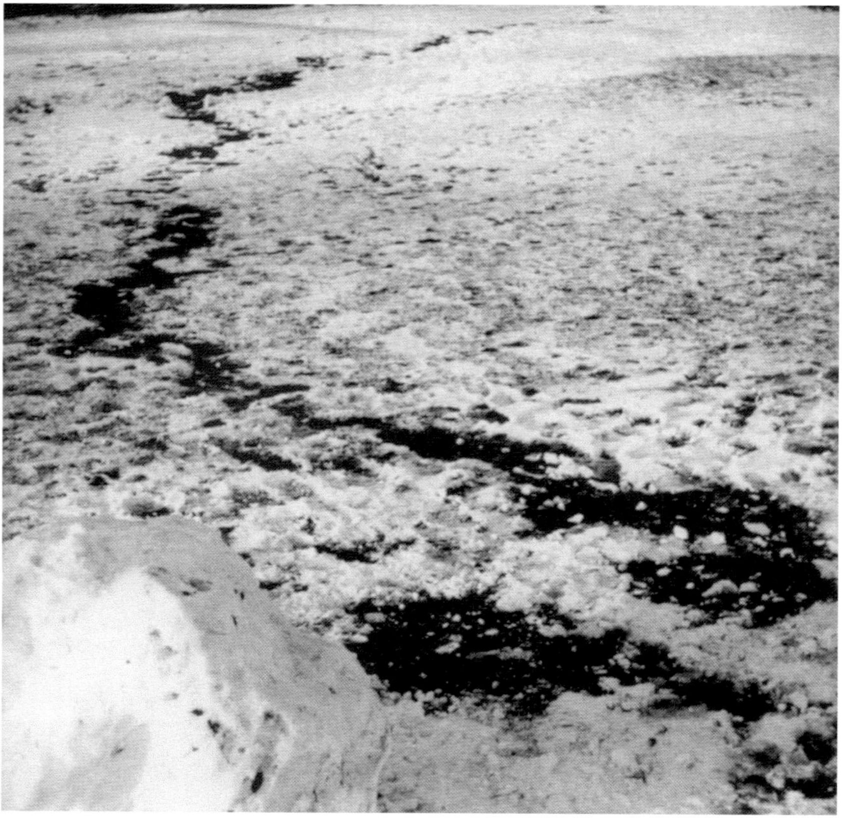

2. Richard Long,
Snowball Track, Bristol, 1964

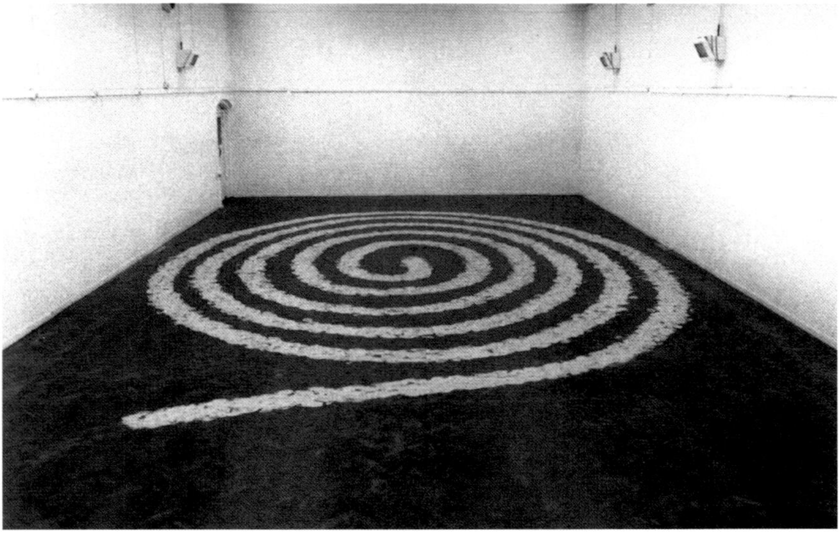

3. Richard Long,
A Line the Length of a Straight Walk from the Bottom to the Top of Silbury Hill, 1970
Installation view at the Whitechapel Gallery, London, 1971

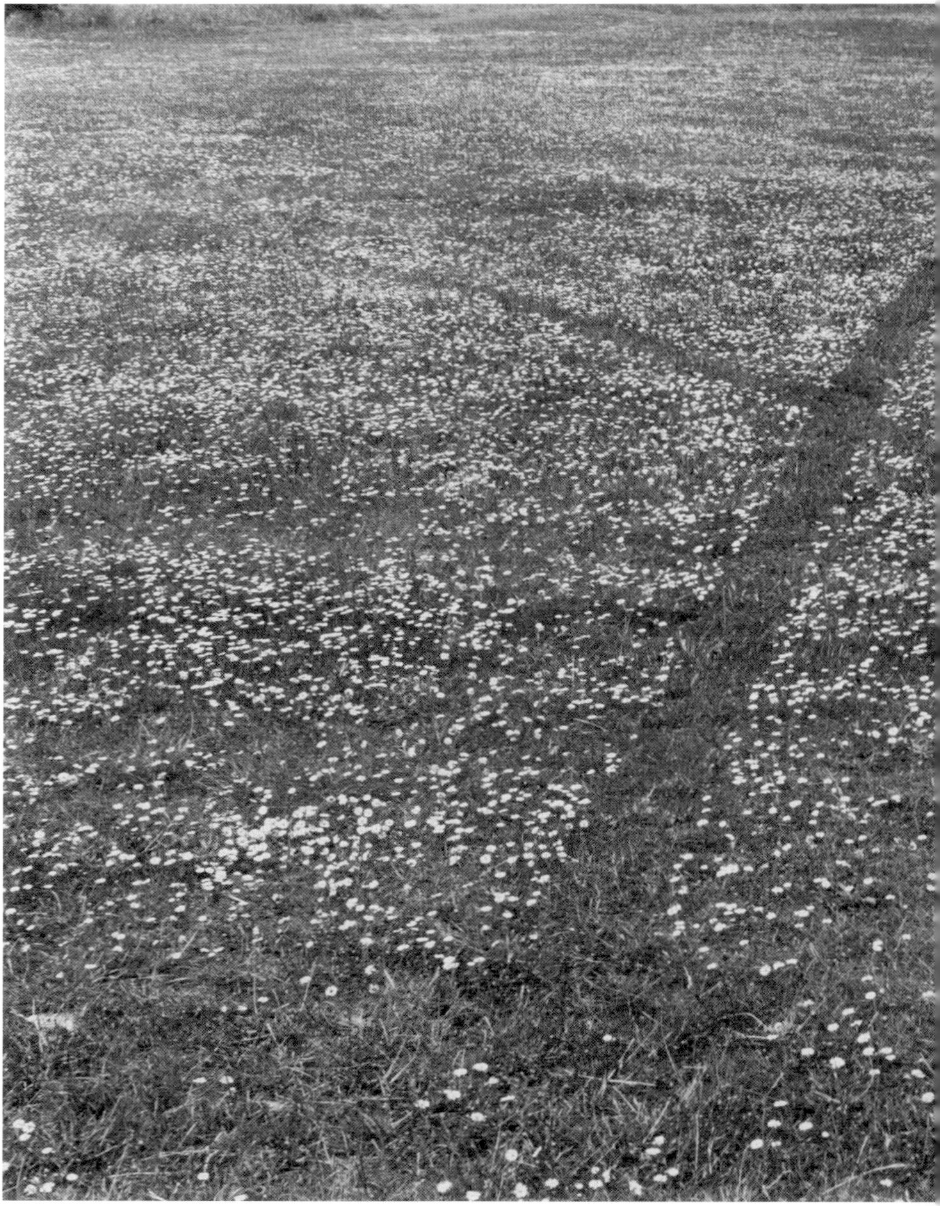

4. Richard Long,
England 1968, 1968

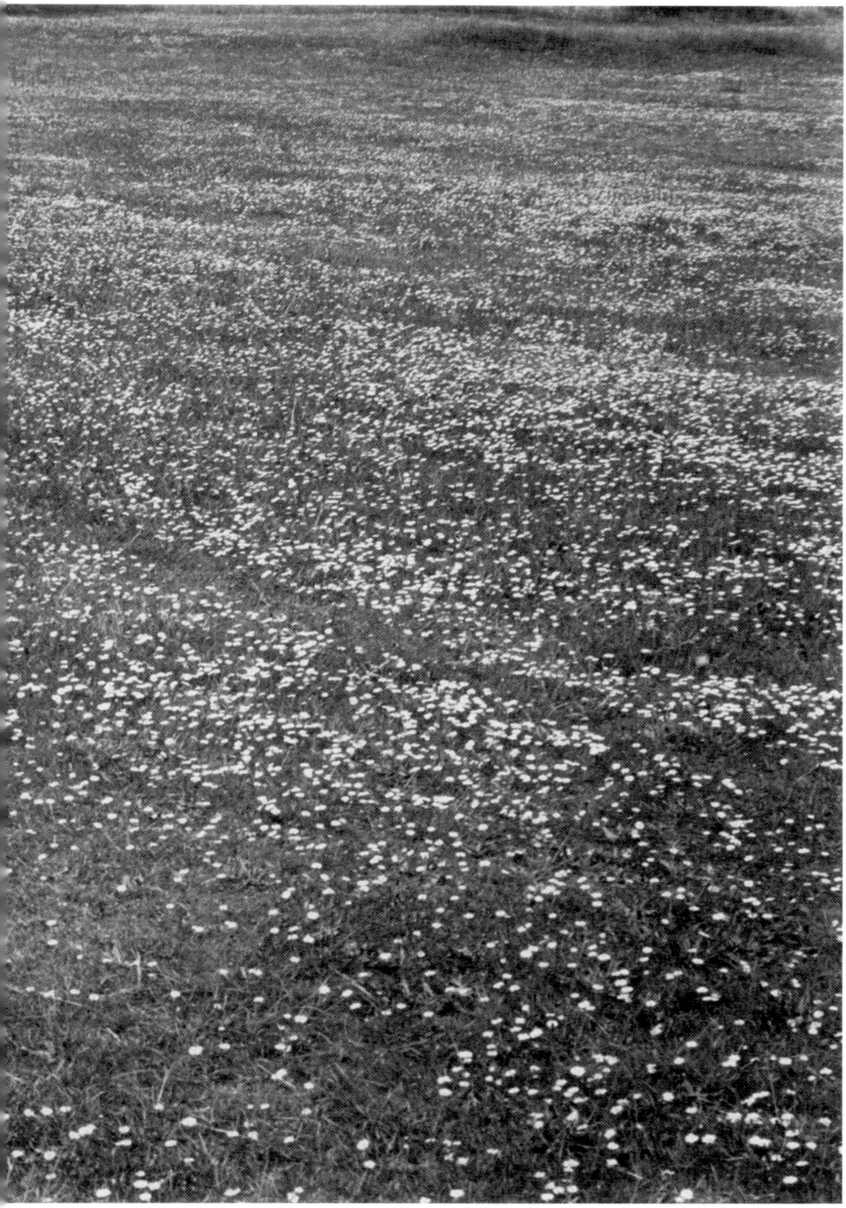

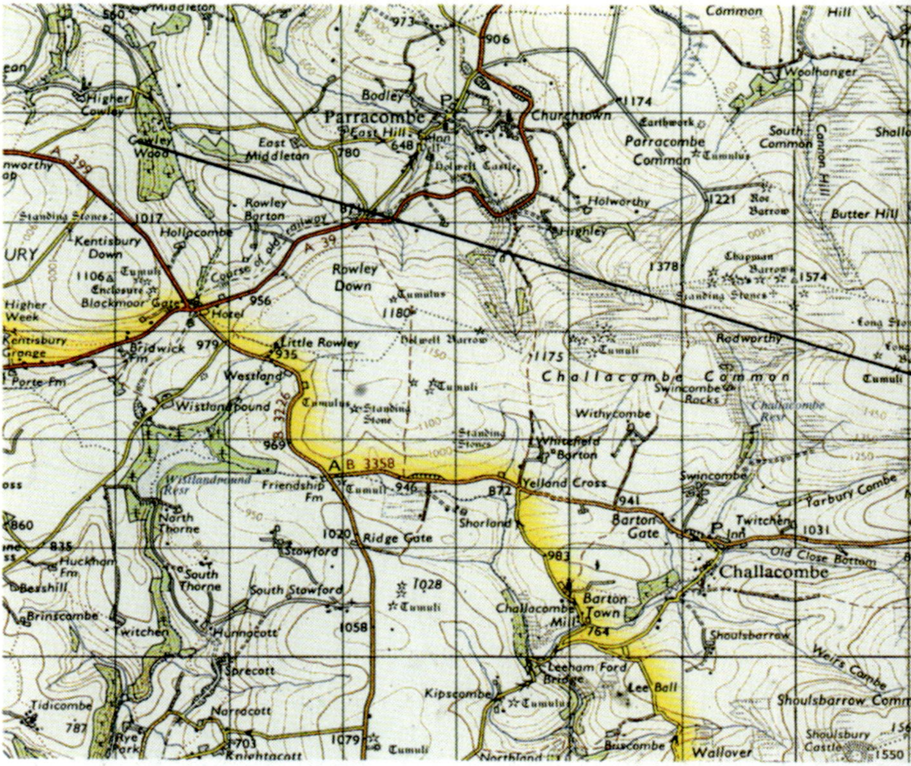

5. Richard Long,
A Ten Mile Walk, England, 1968, 1968,
map and pencil,
64 × 69cm, detail

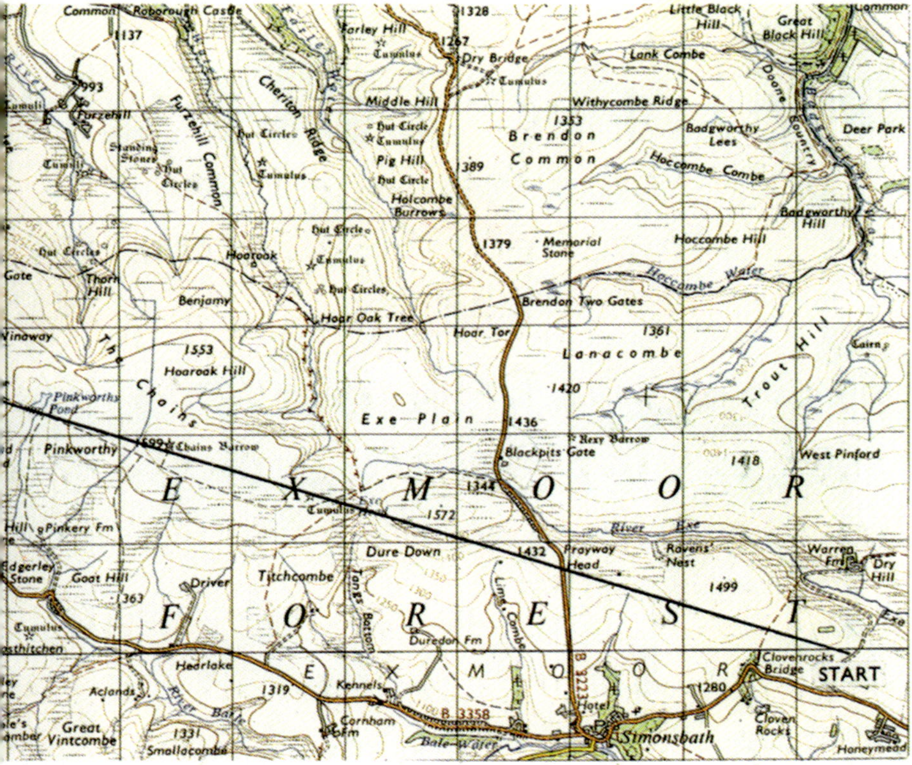

Common
Roborough Castle
1137
993
Furzehill
Furzehill Common
Cheriton Ridge
Standing Stones
Hut Circles
Tumulus
Farley Hill
1328
1267
Dry Bridge
Middle Hill
Hut Circle
Pig Hill
Holcombe Burrows
389
Little Black Hill
Great Black Hill
Common
Lank Combe
Withycombe Ridge
1353
Brendon Common
Badgworthy Lees
Doone Country
Deer Park
Hoccombe Combe
Badgworthy Hill
Hoccombe Hill
1379
Memorial Stone
Hoccombe Water
Brendon Two Gates
Hoar Oak Tree
Hoaroak
Thorn Hill
Benjamy
Gate
Hoar Tor
1361
Lanacombe
Trout Hill
Cairn
1553
Hoaroak Hill
The Chains
Pinkworthy Pond
1420
Exe Plain
1436
Rexy Barrow
Blackpits Gate
1418
West Pinford
Pinkworthy
1599
Chains Barrow
E X M O O R
1344
1572
Pinkery Fm
Dure Down
1432
Prayway Head
River Exe
Ravens' Nest
Warren Fm
Dry Hill
Edgerley Stone
Goat Hill
Driver
Titchcombe
Tangs Bottom
Limecombe
1499
363
F O R E S T
Duredon Fm
Hearlake
Kennels
E X M O O R
B 3223
Clovenrocks Bridge
START
1280
Aclands
1319
Hotel
Simonsbath
Cloven Rocks
Great Vintcombe
1331
Smallacombe
Cornham Fm
B 3358
Barle Water
River Barle
Honeymead

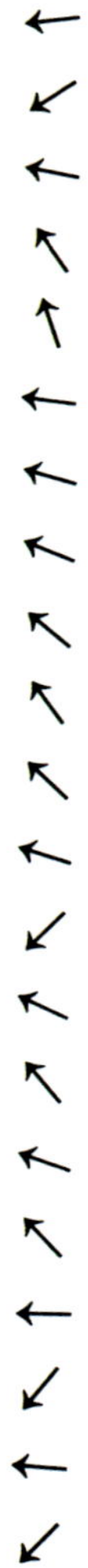

WIND LINE

A STRAIGHT TEN MILE NORTHWARD WALK ON DARTMOOR

1985

6. Richard Long,
Wind Line, 1985

WHITE LIGHT WALK

RED LEAVES OF A JAPANESE MAPLE
ORANGE SUN AT 4 MILES
YELLOW PARSNIPS AT 23 MILES
GREEN RIVER SLIME AT 45 MILES
BLUE EYES OF A CHILD AT 56 MILES
INDIGO JUICE OF A BLACKBERRY AT 69 MILES
VIOLET WILD CYCLAMEN AT 72 MILES

AVON ENGLAND 1987

7. Richard Long,
White Light Walk, 1987

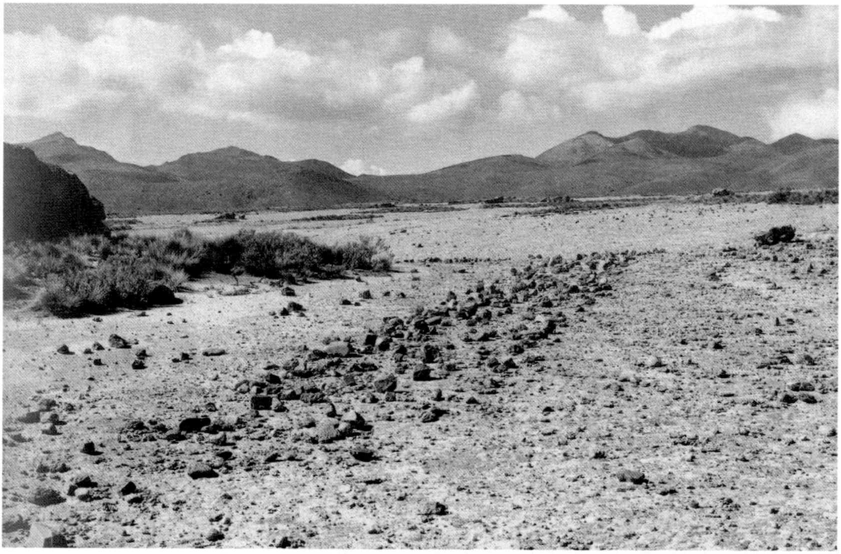

8. Richard Long,
A Line in Bolivia, Kicked Stones, 1981

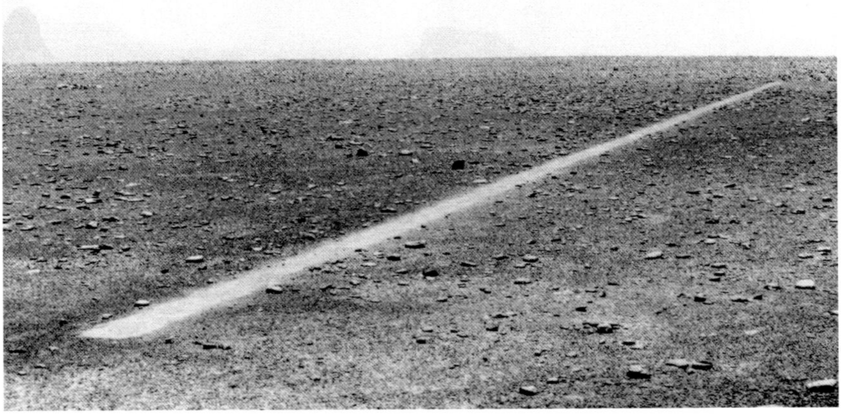

9. Richard Long,
Dusty Boots Line, The Sahara, 1988

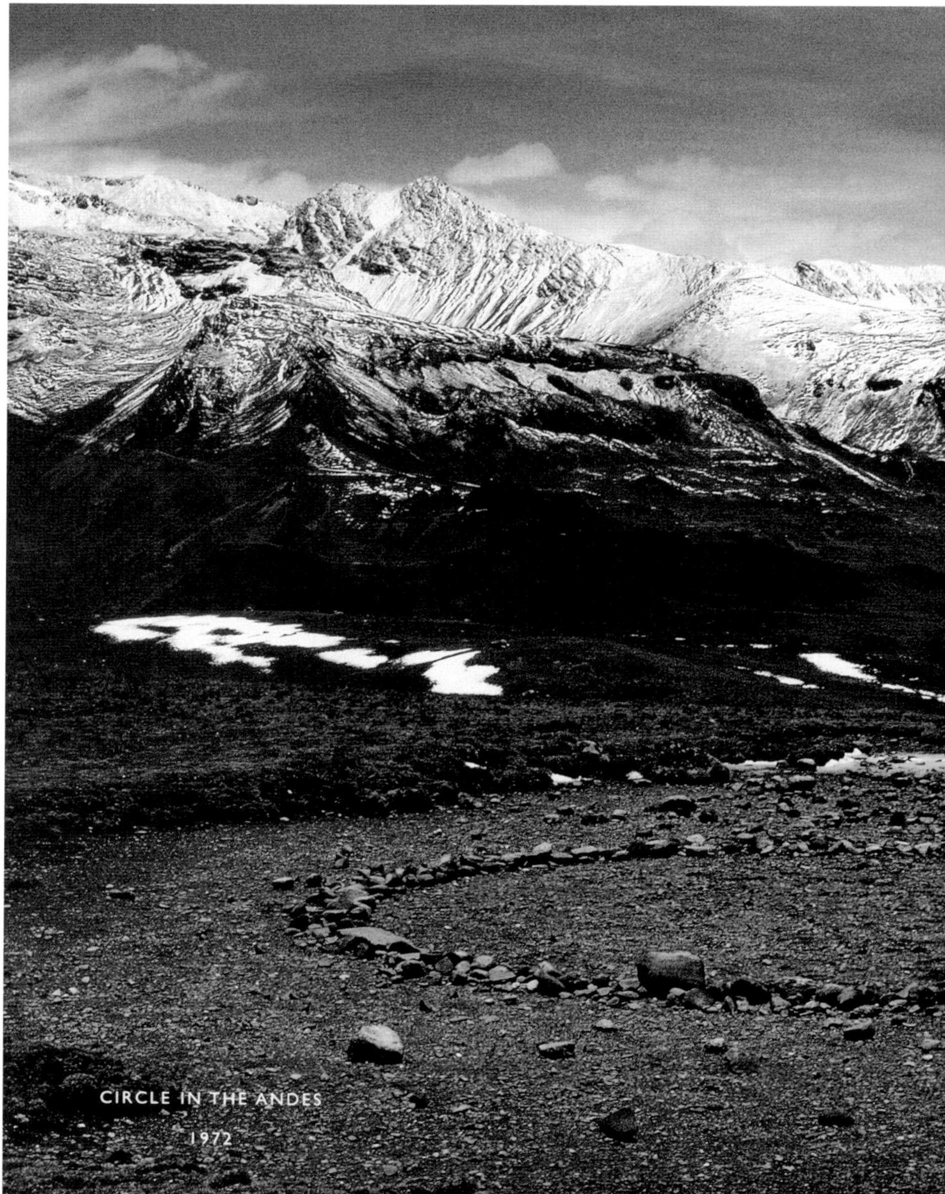

10. Richard Long,
Circle in the Andes, 1972

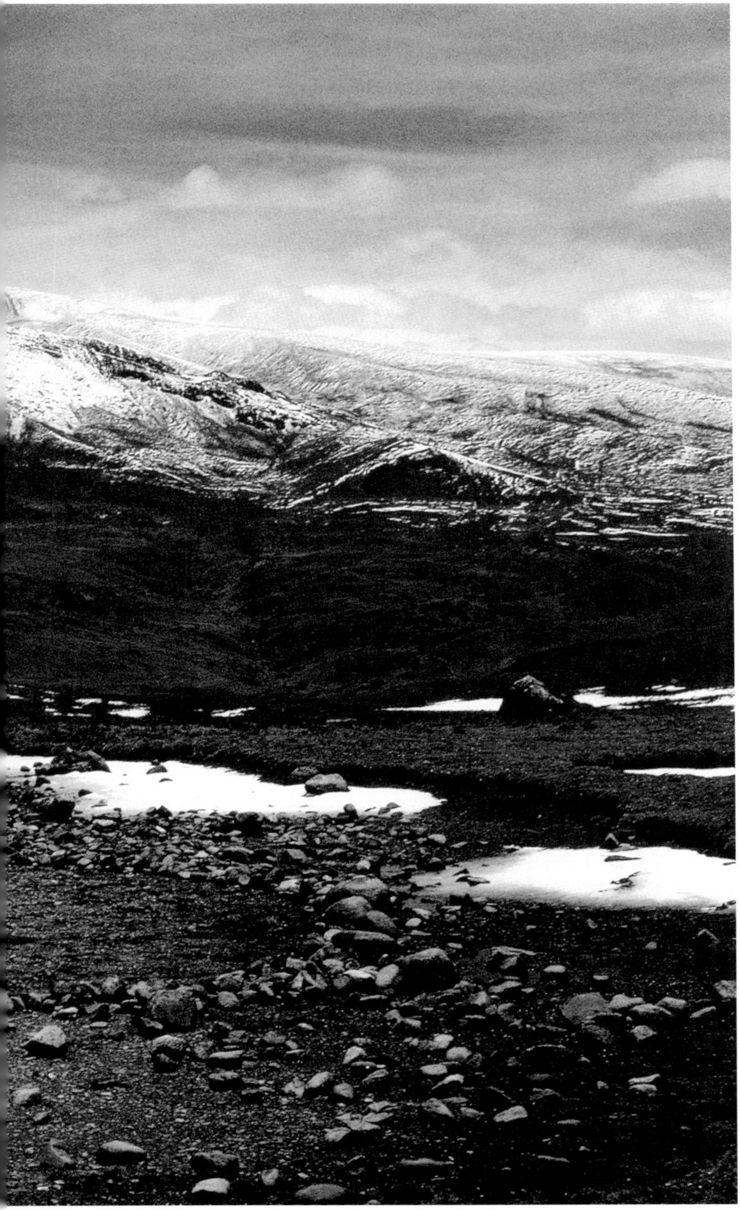

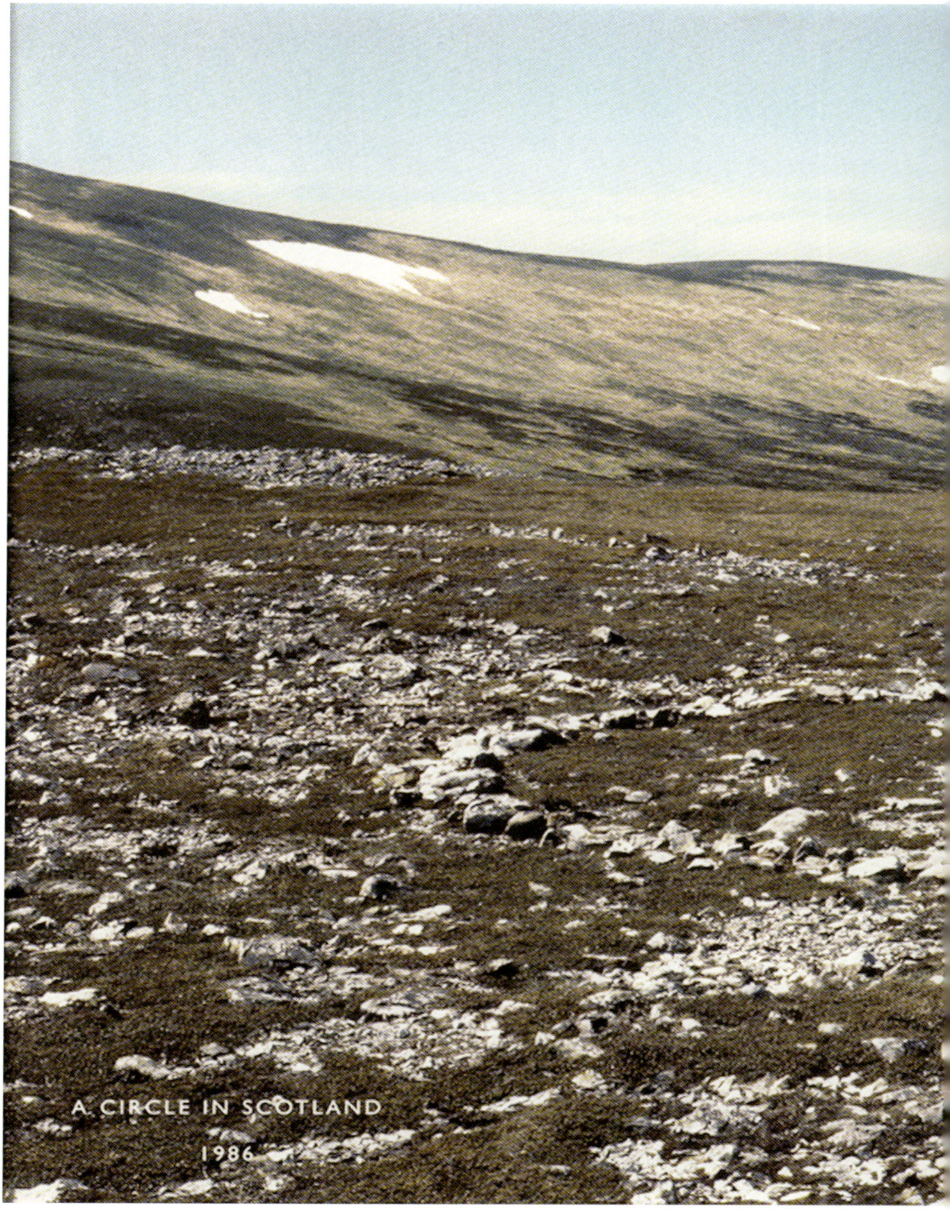

11. Richard Long,
A Circle in Scotland, 1986

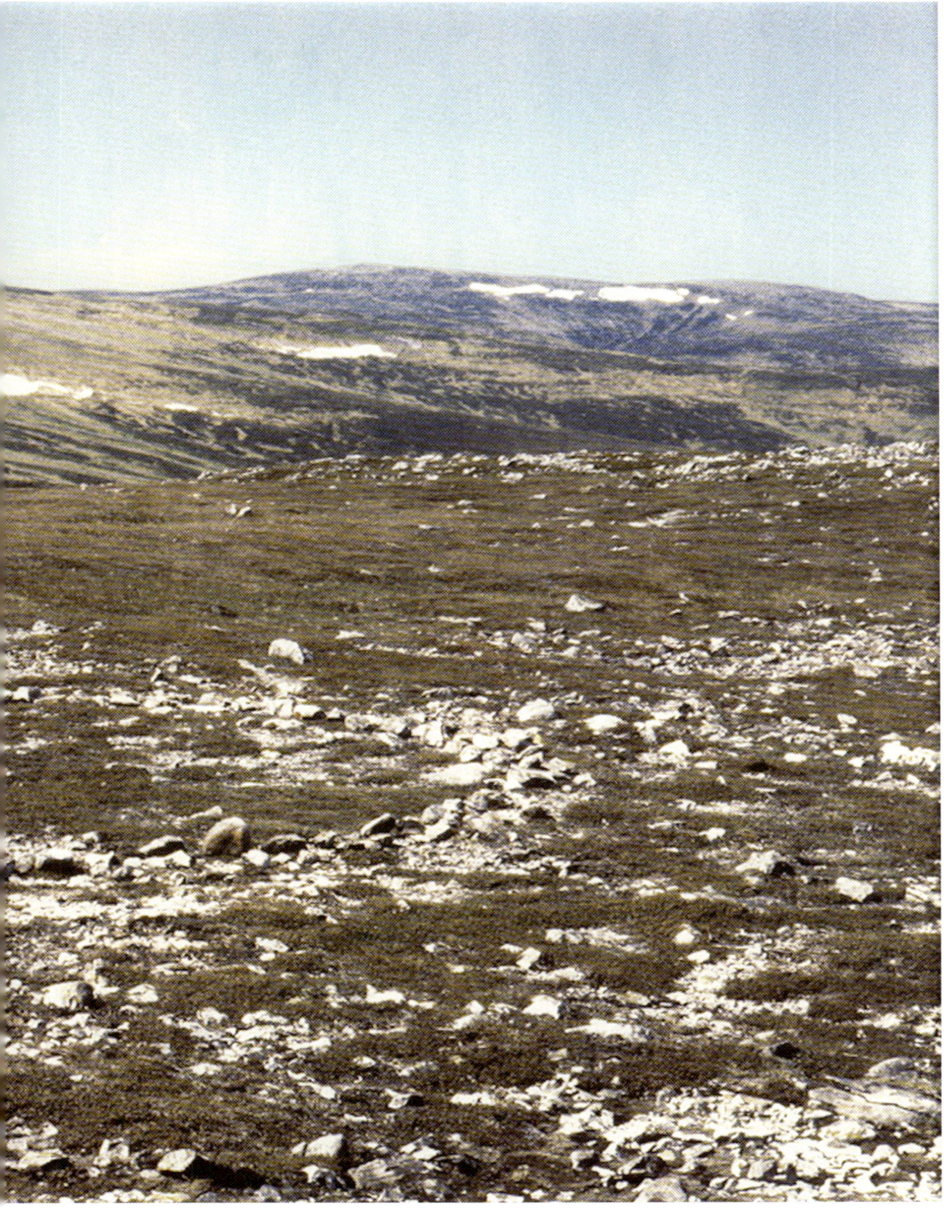

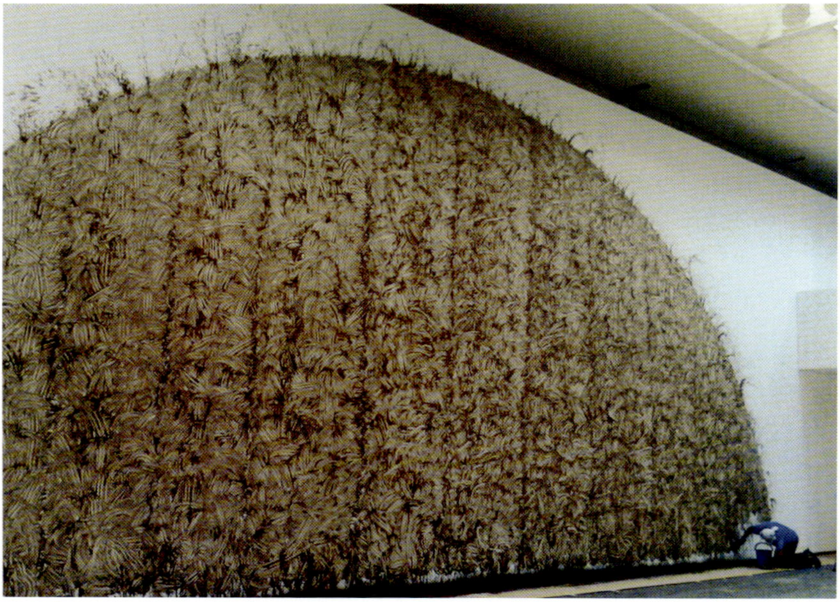

12. Richard Long,
River Avon Mud Arc, 2008
Richard Long installing at Haunch of Venison, Berlin
Photograph © Ben Tufnell

Baudelaire himself famously spoke of the relationship between the loitering *flâneur* — really meaning the artist — and the 'modern' crowd in the following manifesto-like terms:

The crowd is his element, as the air is that of birds and water of fishes. [...] *For the perfect* flâneur, *for the passionate spectator, it is an immense joy to set up house in the heart of the multitude, amid the ebb and flow of movement, in the midst of the fugitive and the infinite. To be away from home and yet to feel oneself everywhere at home; to see the world, to be at the centre of the world, and yet to remain hidden from the world — such are a few of the slightest pleasures of those independent, passionate, impartial natures which the tongue can but clumsily define.*[37]

'To be away from home and yet to feel oneself everywhere at home; to see the world, to be at the centre of the world, and yet to remain hidden from the world' — this could just as well have been a quote from one of Long's (rare) early artist's statements, provided that the emphasis is allowed to shift towards the fact of hiding, of becoming invisible. Solitude and the comforting safety of being as far removed as possible from the 'madding crowd' is of the essence in Long's practice, not least in the artist's immersion in an idealised, depopulated picture of nature.

1967: The Greening of the Art World

Apart from being the year of *A Line Made by Walking*, of the Summer of Love, the Six-Day War and the military coup in Greece, of *Sgt. Pepper's Lonely Hearts Club Band*, the deaths of Benno Ohnesorg and Che Guevara, of Joseph Beuys's founding of the German Student Party in Düsseldorf, the publication in *Artforum* of Mel Bochner's 'Serial Attitude', Sol LeWitt's 'Paragraphs on Conceptual Art' and Michael Fried's 'Art and Objecthood',[38] 1967 also witnessed an epochal event in the development of a global ecological awareness which early Land art clearly (if never directly) responded to: the shipwreck, on 18 March, of the Torrey Canyon supertanker just off the coast of Cornwall in western England — not terribly far from Richard Long's preferred theatre of artistic operations, the idyllic Somerset countryside. Carrying a cargo of 120,000 tons of crude oil, which eventually washed up on 170 miles of Cornish and French coast, the Torrey Canyon caused the first major oil spill in modern history. This being a first, many improvised emergency measures attempted to contain the disaster actually made matters worse: many of the chemical dispersants that were subsequently sprayed onto the oil slicks were more lethal for the wildlife affected than the actual oil. Two years later, the United States witnessed a similarly horrific natural disaster, the Santa Barbara Oil Spill off the coast of Southern California, providing yet more invective to the budding environmental movement. And in 1971, W. Eugene Smith's harrowing photo-essay *Minamata* brought the so-called 'Minamata disease' to worldwide attention — an instance of methylmercury poisoning which occurred in the Japanese city of Minamata due to the industrial discharge of mercury into the rivers and coastal waters of Kumamoto Prefecture, resulting in the severe deformations and premature deaths of over six-hundred people.

Within a decade book-ended by two landmark publications that helped to lodge ecological issues at the centre of public awareness — Rachel Carson's *Silent Spring* from 1962 and the Club of Rome's *Limits to Growth* from 1972[39] — the year 1967 signalled the advent of environmental awareness as one of the defining socio-political forces for years to come (although it was really only the organisation, on 22 April 1970, of the world's first Earth Day that catapulted environmentalism from the margins into the mainstream of post-industrial Western society).[40] It is no coincidence that 1967 also saw the birth of Land and/or Environmental art, which, as an early offshoot of Conceptual art, was deeply implicated in the latter movement's critique of production. Indeed, Conceptual art's critique of production and productivism was a two-pronged affair, one aspect of which was more narrowly art historical in temperament, best expressed in Lawrence Weiner's famous dictum from 1969, 'I do not mind objects, but I do not care to make them', and by the tenth of Sol LeWitt's 'Sentences on Conceptual Art' (1969), 'All ideas need not be made physical'.[41] In that same year Douglas Huebler also claimed that 'the world is full of objects, more or less interesting; I do not wish to add any more'; and John Baldessari asked himself the question: 'The world has too much art — I have made too many objects — What to do?'[42] The other key aspect of Conceptual art was more broadly informed by the culture of contestation and student dissent from which the movement partly emerged, aimed more specifically at a critique of the materialist values of consumer society and the capitalist logic of overproduction — a transformative critique of everyday life, in short, in which everyday life itself would be salvaged from the onslaught of its materialist reduction to a mere ritual of producing and consuming, of buying and selling.

The notion of the 'rehabilitation of everyday life' is an allusion to the informal motto of Henri Lefebvre's *Critique of Everyday Life*, first published in 1947 and one of the defining inspirations, twenty years later, for the French student revolt of the late 1960s: 'Man must be everyday, or he will not be at all.'[43] The politics of early Conceptual art were clearly indebted to this defiant reappraisal of the quotidian as a major source of aesthetic pleasure — with supposedly revolutionary political implications. Richard Long's choice of material for something as banal and prosaic (indeed, as pedestrian) as plain walking must equally be viewed within this context of the political aestheticisation of everyday life. Lefebvre's critique of the commodification of everyday life is reflected, finally, in Conceptual art's lofty contempt for the artwork as commodity, leading many early practicioners of the movement to imagine that they could effectively operate outside the commercial system of art — a fantasy shared by many Land artists engaging in all kinds of emphatically commodification-resistant artistic activity.

Jan Dibbets, who in 1966 began to call himself a *dématerialisateur*, in 1968 released a statement that ended on the following provocative high note, and included an unwitting nod to the Marxist theory of alienation: 'Sell my work? To sell isn't part of the art. Maybe there will be people idiotic enough to buy what they could make themselves. So much the worse for them.' See also Carl Andre's statement, made in the same year, on the occasion of an outdoor exhibition in Windham College, Vermont: 'the hay of course [referring to the material used to make his sculpture *Joint*, from 1968] is going to break down and gradually disappear. But since I am not making a piece of sculpture for sale, it never enters the property state.'[44] It is worth adding, finally, that the critique of consumer society in which so much vanguard art of the time was rooted also entailed a critique of *speed*, of the process of acceleration to which man was subjected in the industrial regime of mechanisation and overproduction.

Though of course never explicitly couched in these terms, *A Line Made by Walking* and much of Long's subsequent work clearly belong to this anti-productivist, anti-commodity tradition in twentieth-century art. It may well be the closest art ever came to the programmatic dissolution, so eagerly desired by so much modern art, of *aesthetics* into *ethics*: in turning walking itself into an originary art form, into his signature method of art-making, Long literally pulled out of the Fordist chain of production, thereby automatically minimising his impact on the natural environment in which he walked —

the expanded studio in which his practice was to take shape in the decades to come. Following this impulse, many of the later driftwood circles, mud drawings and stone lines simply came out of 'sketches' first made in situ, during his walks across stone-strewn terrain. In this sense, and precisely because it is set in the relatively unspoiled 'natural' world outside the perimeters of traditional art production, the work functions as an early harbinger of the gradual 'greening' of the art world which continues to this day. The critical impetus behind much of Long's work, and certainly behind *A Line Made by Walking*, could be traced back to the ecosophical dictum 'Take only photographs, leave only footprints' — one of the main rules of conduct eschewed by the Sierra Club, the oldest, largest and most influential grassroots environmental organisation in the United States. (The slogan, incidentally, also greets every visitor to the personal website of Long's long-time travelling companion Hamish Fulton.)[45]

This, of course, is precisely where Environmental art in the UK has always fancied itself radically different from the much more spectacular brand of Land or Earth art practised in North America at around the same time. And this is where the work of Fulton and Long, as well as of others such as Ian Hamilton Finlay, Andy Goldsworthy and Peter Hutchinson, has been open to occasional alignment with the more explicitly politicised non-object-based art practices of British groups and artists such as Keith Arnatt, Art & Language, Victor Burgin and the like. Much has been written about the fundamental differences between North American Land art and British (or more broadly European) Environmental art, and *A Line Made by Walking* certainly epitomises many of these more glaring divergences, between an aggressive, macho ethic (if, and this is crucial here, that term 'macho ethic' can be used at all) of intrusion ('penetration'), conquest and domination, on the one hand, and a much gentler, unassuming ethos of ecological accommodation, on the other; between, say, Michael Heizer's *Double Negative* (1969—70), which is really a 'line made by bulldozing', and Richard Long's *A Line Made by Walking*. A penchant towards monumentalism (in, for example, Heizer or Walter De Maria) and sheer entropic violence (in Robert Smithson) seems to have characterised much art made on one side of the Atlantic, while the cultivation of self-effacement and humility in the face of nature and the landscape was the dominant force on the other.

This has long been a problematic simplification, to say the least, and some of the harsher criticisms of the aforementioned Environmental artists' seemingly innocuous landscape art actually concern its illusory innocence. Some critics have objected to the perceived naivety of Environmental art's ethical claims in these works in particular, noting that non-production does not automatically mean non-intervention — in fact, its effects may turn out to be the more toxic or noxious ones. Rebecca Solnit even goes as far as to call aspects of Long's work a neo-colonially inflected form of high-handed tourism:

Long likes places where nothing seems to have broken the connection to the ancient past, so buildings, people and other traces of the present or recent past rarely appear. His work revises the British tradition of country walks while representing its most enchanting and problematic faces. He has gone to Australia, the Himalayas and the Bolivian Andes to make his work, and the idea that all these places can be assimilated into a thoroughly English experience smacks of colonialism or at least high-handed tourism. It raises once again the perils of forgetting that the rural walk is a culturally specific practice, and though it may be a civil, gentle thing in itself, imposing its values elsewhere is not.[46]

All in all, it is important to appreciate the true economic rationale of the Atlantic divide in Land and Environmental art, for the crucial term in North American Land art is really 'ownership' — one has to *own* the land (or at least unimaginably vast stretches of it) to be able to do to it what Heizer, De Maria and Smithson did, or at least have privileged access to large swathes of land owned by someone else. The proverbial semantic triangle of North American Land art, then, revolves around land (i.e. the actual expanse), money (the means of acquiring part of the expanse) and monumentalism (in that the sheer magnitude of the expanse requires a different logic of scaling in conceiving and actually executing the artwork). And the inclusion of money as a cardinal term in this equation of course also meant that these artists quickly experienced greater difficulty in toeing the party line, however perfunctorily, of the emancipatory rhetoric espoused by avant-garde art in the late 1960s and early 70s. Finally, spaces such as the New Mexico desert or the Utah salt flats simply do not exist in Britain. Discussing the difference between the earth works being made in the United States and in England, Carl Andre famously noted, in an interview published in *Avalanche* in the autumn of 1970, that 'Great Britain is one big open-air earth work already'.[47] This meant that British artists had to approach the terrain with greater subtlety and (inevitably in the absence of something like a vast virgin wilderness) modesty — virtues that had long been associated with the British national psyche, but less so with the American.

This is not to say that scale was never a consideration in British Environmental art: a thousand-mile-long walk across Great Britain, as in Long's *A Thousand Miles A Thousand Hours A Clockwise Walk in England Summer 1974* (1974) could be called the biggest artwork ever made, and the proposed prehistoric 'precedents' of a specifically British Land art tradition certainly rank among either the world's largest sculptural ensembles (as in Stonehenge) or the world's largest drawings (as in the White Horse of Uffington).[48] The straight or meandering lines of Long's many walks can be superimposed on any landscape, on any terrain — hence Solnit's charge of neo-colonial intrusion — and the idea of the potentially limitless scale of such an artwork, of an artwork so large that it can only unfold over time (i.e. in the 'fourth dimension' of art that *is* time),[49] was only first opened up by the 'discovery' of walking as an art form, of its linear path as a sculptural inscription, however fleeting, in the surface of the Earth. And in choosing the simple act of walking the earth (whether in lines or in circles) as the basis of his artistic life, Long has foregrounded time as an essential fourth element in his work, indispensable to the possibility of its limitless scale, among other things. In an early artist statement, he noted that 'my art has the themes of materials, ideas, movement, time'[50] — time being that which allows for the movement of both ideas and materials across a space of principled limitlessness.

The Antics of Disappearance (Indifference and Repetition)

To repeat is to behave in a certain manner, but in relation to something unique or singular which has no equal or equivalent.
— Gilles Deleuze, *Difference and Repetition*[51]

Whether walking a straight line up and down a field in Surrey or across the Nazca Desert in Peru, or simply walking in circles in the snow-covered Italian Alps (*Footprint Circle*, 1989) or in the dust of Turkish Anatolia (*Walking a Circle in Dust*, 1989), Long's predilection for straight lines and perfect circles is not only a matter of formal taste and Minimalist aesthetics, but is clearly also informed by modern art's long-standing historical interest in compulsion, repetition and the ritual emptying out of the repetitive gesture — voiding, avoidance, the void — as both the means and ends of art-making. In this sense, *A Line Made by*

Walking, a tracing made by literally pacing up and down the same path in an empty field — an 'absence' or void *produced* by depersonalised repetitive behaviour — and the various circular walks that followed soon after very much belong to an era in art dominated by the spirit of John Cage and his cohorts. They did much to popularise and introduce ideas taken from Zen Buddhism and Taoism, known for their emphasis on the epistemological virtues of repetition, emptiness, ellipsis, effacement and boredom, into the cultural imagination of Western art — all of which added up to a particularly welcome, liberating antidote to the progress-mad, teleological productivist ethic so pervasive in the West at the time. Needless to say, the dominance of this particular ethic was also, and just as effectively, challenged from *within* the realm of that Western cultural imagination. From the mid 1960s onwards, the grandiose ideological complex of Enlightenment values, historical progress, *telos* and Western universalism was gradually being dismantled by a small group of theorists and thinkers working in the adjoining fields of cultural history, linguistics and literary theory, (political) philosophy and structural anthropology, such as Louis Althusser, Roland Barthes, Jacques Derrida, Michel Foucault, Jacques Lacan, Claude Lévi-Strauss and, a little bit later, Jean-François Lyotard. Barthes, Derrida and Foucault were especially influential, and quickly made their mark on the international arts scene, not least because of their interest in ideas of dissolution and disappearance — of *dematerialisation*. Foucault, who later in life also experienced his own Zen Buddhist revelation, perhaps sensed the constructive quality of dematerialisation most keenly when he concluded *The Order of Things* (1966) with the following classic vision of philosophy's future, conjuring images seemingly straight out of the early Environmental art canon: 'one can certainly wager that man would be erased, like a face drawn in sand at the edge of the sea'.[52] Not surprisingly, Richard Long also made his fair share of ephemeral artworks, sometimes no more than lines drawn in the sand, by the edge of a river or sea. It is interesting to note here that Foucault's vision of the disappearance of man (and of his many manifestations, such as the male subject, the artist, the author, etc.) takes on a high-pitched *aesthetic* tone: this disappearance of man is presaged by that of an *artwork*, the very meaning of which resides in its irreversible erasure. Does this mean, finally, that the projected disappearance of man, as an artistic gesture in itself, is inextricably linked to the *appearance of the artist*?

Indeed Long did not escape John Cage's influence, and, as he has pointed out, seeing Cage lecture and perform in London in 1966 was a decisive, formative experience. Certainly, a performance of Cage's notorious 1952 composition *4'33"* (allegedly inspired by seeing an exhibition of Rauschenberg's all-white canvases at Black Mountain College, among them the erased de Kooning referred to previously)[53] must have alerted any aspiring young artist in this transitional period to the immense, uncharted artistic possibilities of gestural non-production, of ritualised withdrawal — as would any of Cage's later lectures on the art of mushroom picking. In *A Line Made by Walking*, this Zen-styled disappearing act — Long has called 'empty space' (that is to say, space without people, including the artist himself) the only true subject of his work[54] — was enacted by way of a Zen-like exercise in *repetition*.

Repetition had become a notable trope in art-making a few years before, both in the field of visual arts and of music. In art, as early as 1963, Andy Warhol had professed his desire to become a machine, and the simultaneous development in sculpture known as Minimalism quickly delivered the longed-for serial methodology of the machine. Warhol's deadpan glorification of the machine aesthetic and subsequent reconfiguration of art as a conveyor belt-driven business proposition (which led him to rename his studio 'The Factory') relates back to the ecstasy of production and consumer fever characteristic of the early 1960s, which Conceptual art was shortly thereafter to criticise with such fiery enthusiasm. The work of Sol LeWitt is a pivotal link in this chain of events, as it appeared as invested in the fantasy of a theoretically limitless, serial production of art as it was in the critique of (re-)production as such. In the field of music, the very term 'Minimalism' was only introduced in 1968 by Michael Nyman, having already been established as a valid art-historical term. However, serialism as a productive, disciplinary methodology had long been recognised in the field of music by the time 'systems art' emerged in the early 1960s. Serialism's obsession with counting and measurements (most ostensibly in the work of Mel Bochner and On Kawara) also resonates in Long's walks, which are often founded on the twinned tactic of measuring (the landscape) and counting (the artist's steps as a way of measuring it). Repetition had, in the meantime, also appeared as a mighty force in the theatre of the absurd, and the influence of Samuel Beckett — a much darker cloud than Cage's naturally sunny disposition — could likewise be discerned in much cultural activity of the time. These matters were in the exact air that so much art was trying to resemble or emulate. 'Air art' — the title, incidentally, of an exhibition organised in 1968 by Willoughby Sharp — as a particularly symbolic offshoot of Land and Environmental art, was practised by Robert Morris (see his *Steam* from 1967), Hans Haacke (*Condensation Cube*, 1965) and Christo (*5,600 Cubicmeter Package*, 1968), among others. Robert Barry's series of 'inert gas release' performances, during which he released the likes of krypton, xenon, argon and helium into the Californian desert air, and Art & Language's tellingly titled 'Air Conditioning' show in New York in 1972, prophesied in Michael Baldwin's *Remarks on Air-Conditioning: An Extravaganza of Blandness* (1967), both illustrate to what extent the ethereal was simply 'in the air', even among the more orthodox Conceptualists. Long's 'wind line' works are equally part of this history of extreme vaporisation. One such 'drawing', as mentioned earlier, consists of 21 arrows that trace the changing wind direction during a straight ten-mile northward walk on Dartmoor; another, *Wind Line Across England* (1986), is a drawing/text piece of fourteen rotating arrows, the explanatory text underneath which reads: 'A 130 mile walk in 3 1/2 days from the Irish Sea coast to the North Sea coast / The wind direction at each coast and at every ten miles along the way.' Beckettian repetition in turn engendered the existential angst and boredom that is at the heart of much early performance art of the era, whether authentically (in so far as it is possible to authenticate these performances as such) or ironically. An example of the non-ironic position can be found in Bruce Nauman's work from the late 1960s, with its repetitive, monomaniacal, studio-bound gestures, which presage a later interest in the macabre business of torture and political imprisonment, showing the artist as a caged, neurotic animal rather than as an enlightened sadhu. In contrast, a certain brand of irony seems to be more present in the work of On Kawara and John Baldessari. In a seminal piece from 1971 titled *I Will Not Make Any More Boring Art*, Baldessari instructed his students at the Nova Scotia College of Art and Design (one of the nerve centres of Conceptual art) to endlessly reiterate the prohibitive mantra 'I will not make any more boring art'.

Boredom and its origin in compulsive repetition as a dual site of transgressive provocations, then — is this not precisely what led Gilles Deleuze to assert that 'in every respect, repetition is a transgression'?[55] Do we not encounter here, in the transgressive illogic of repetition, 'the logos of the solitary and the singular (which) puts law into question and denounces its nominal or general character in favor of a more profound and more artistic reality'?[56] Indeed, in *Difference and Repetition*, originally published in 1968 and from which the above quotes are taken, Deleuze crucially distinguished two different languages: 'the language of science, dominated by the symbol of equality, in which each term may be replaced by others; and lyrical language, in which every term is irreplaceable and can only be repeated'.[57] And whereas 'generality belongs to the order of laws' — the entities that govern both science and the language of science — 'if repetition is possible, it is due to miracle rather than to law'. In fact, he continues:

It is against the law: against the similar form and the equivalent content of law. If repetition can be found, even in nature, it is in the name of a power which affirms itself against the law, which works underneath laws, perhaps superior to laws. If repetition exists, it expresses at once a singularity opposed to the general, a universality opposed to the particular, a distinctive opposed to the ordinary, an instantaneity opposed to variation and an eternity opposed to permanence.

Deleuze draws on both Friedrich Nietzsche's rhapsodic figure of the eternal return — promulgated most exhaustively in his *Thus Spoke Zarathustra* (1885), itself replete with all kinds of echoes, recursions and reiterations meant to invoke the spirit of inebriation which permeates the whole of Zarathustra's droning gospel — and Karl Marx's notion of the tragicomic in the 'repetition' of history to conclude that 'repetition belongs to humour and irony; it is by nature transgression or exception, always revealing a singularity opposed to the particulars subsumed under laws, a universal opposed to the generalities which give rise to laws'.[58]

Humour and irony may not be directly discernible in *A Line Made by Walking*, but there is a definite quality of profound dumbness (literally so, as its silence is so palpable) to the work that it seems to share with certain notions of the deadpan which can be associated with the work of Samuel Beckett. And Beckett greatly admired the undisputed master of deadpan, Buster Keaton, whom I imagine would have liked *A Line Made by Walking* very much. Furthermore, the dumbness of Long's repetitive gesture has a decidedly comic (if not necessarily humorous) undertone that may also be associated with (caged) animal behaviour — or, more lugubriously perhaps, with the death drive as theorised in Freud's *Beyond the Pleasure Principle* (1920), in which the tragicomic essence of human existence is recast as an irresolvable tug of war between eros and thanatos.[59] In this regard as well, repetition can be viewed as a source of both pleasure (eros, comedy) and discomfort (thanatos, tragedy). It is something we seek out as well as avoid — an ambiguity cleverly mined in so much comedy revolving around the eternal return of pain, such as 1920s slapstick movies, with their endless car chases and mechanical ministrations of bodily harm.

That deadpan humour is no stranger to oriental wisdom is something that can be easily appreciated by even the most casual reading of such Taoist classics as the *Tao Te Ching* or the *Hagakure Analects* (better known as *The Way of the Samurai*). I have often considered the possibility that the Buddhist gesture of sweeping up a sand drawing or mandala that took hours, days, weeks to make is in fact the expression of an acquired taste in practical joking.[60] The ludic dimension in Long's work is obviously connected to repetition, but also to its prosaic 'silence' (that of the knowing smirk instead of the austerely pursed lips) and to the sheer enjoyment of evaporation, of the irreversible fact of its disappearance into thin air — like laughter itself. Here, his work may be said to intersect with that of Gilbert & George (whose first 'singing sculpture' performance took place at St. Martin's School of Art in London in 1969) as well as with that of Baldessari and Huebler, or a more light-hearted Bas

Jan Ader — artists who did not deem the rigour of Conceptual art irreconcilable with comedy, and whose work perhaps for this very reason has enjoyed a remarkable revaluation in recent years.

The 'art of disappearance' was an overarching concern uniting many (often literally escapist) artistic practices of the late 1960s and early 70s, and, some dramatic cases notwithstanding, the obsession with elision, deletion, omission, withdrawal and vanishing has produced many hilarious artworks. Now comedy may not always have been the primary goal of many of these straight-faced works, but it is hard to imagine there was no irony involved in some of the more outrageous proposals made in this heady time of boundless experimentation, during which the individual was so often encouraged to get back in touch with his or her 'inner child' — and doesn't much child's play revolve, in essence, around either compulsive repetition or hide-and-seek? Robert Barry's *Closed Gallery Piece* from 1969 is a fine example of the explosive conflation of absurd humour, on the one hand, and the 'aesthetics of disappearance' (and wholesale cultural obsession with Cagean, if not necessarily Duchampian, silence and nothingness), on the other: during a whole month in the winter of 1969, the artist's contribution to the Art & Project exhibition programme in Amsterdam consisted of a notice stuck to the door of the gallery stating 'the gallery will be closed during the exhibition'. British Conceptual art pioneer Keith Arnatt — whose early forays into Land art had consisted of his digging holes, the physical realisation of Long's inscription of disappearance into the surface of the earth — titled one of his works *Is it possible for me to do nothing as my contribution to this exhibition?* (1970), and stoically mused, in the title of a postcard work, on the possibility of *Art as an Act of Omission* (1971).[61] In wondering whether 'doing nothing' could possibly constitute the crux of his artistic practice, Arnatt not only spoke of boredom, anomie, non-production and the orientalist romance of Taoist or Zen

Buddhist withdrawal, he also responded to the Situationist call to 'never work' — *ne travaillez jamais* was one of the better-known graffiti slogans on the walls of the Sorbonne during the spring of 1968. That same year, Arnatt conducted his first experiments with burying people rather than merely digging holes, a shift which would eventually lead to what is perhaps his best known artwork, *Self-Burial (In Nine Stages)*, 1969 (fig.18), a series of nine photographs which show the artist facing the camera, progressively disappearing into the ground. Explaining his motivation for this particular non-performance piece, Arnatt stated in 1979, on the occasion of an exhibition curated by Gerry Schum at the Stedelijk Museum in Amsterdam, that 'it was originally made as a comment upon the notion of the "disappearance of the art object". It seemed a logical corollary that the artist should also disappear.'[62] Let us compare this with the following passage taken from Robert Walser's short story 'The Walk' (1917): 'Left of the country road here, a foundry full of workmen and industry cause a noticeable disturbance. In recognition of this I am honestly ashamed to be merely out for a walk while so many others drudge and labour.'[63]

The aforementioned examples of John Baldessari's work (especially the repetitive *I Will Not Make Any More Boring Art*) indicate why he has been in practically every single exhibition about the uses of humour in art since he decided to incinerate his painterly output in 1970; besides, his singing of Sol LeWitt's fabled 'Sentences on Conceptual Art' is not just a funny work, but also demonstrates the humour of LeWitt's pseudo-parodic manifesto itself. Earlier on, in 1958, Yves Klein had exhibited the empty contents of Iris Clert's Parisian gallery in *Le Vide* (*The Void*), which was humorously rebuked two years later by Arman's *Le Plein* (*Full-Up*) two years later (the two artists had in fact met in a martial arts club). Klein's magisterially advertised

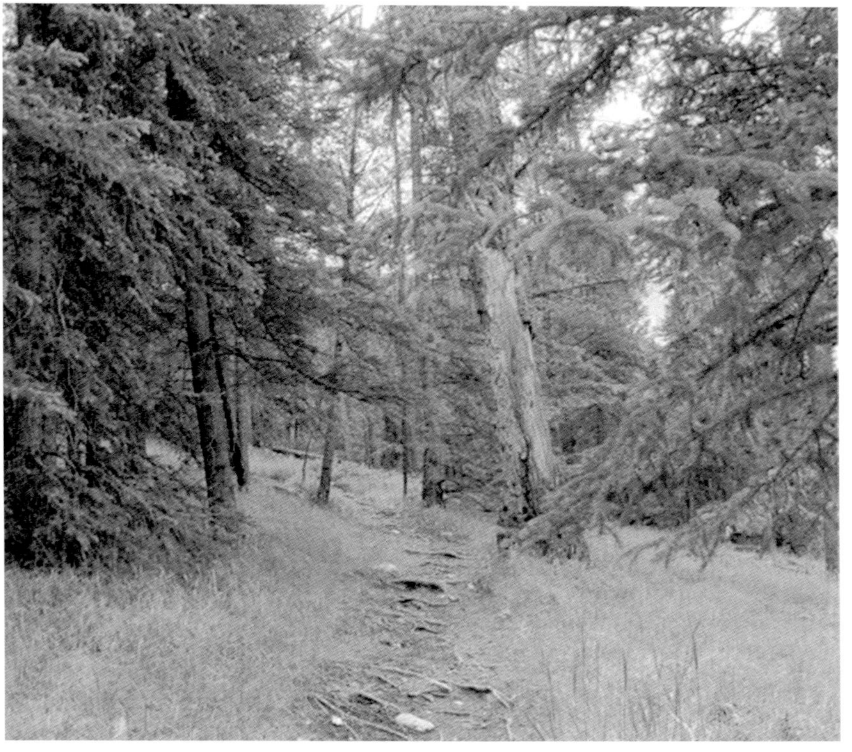

13—14. Janet Cardiff,
Forest Walk, 1991,
audio walk, 12min
Banff Centre for the Arts, Canadian Artist
in Residence Program

Image courtesy of the artist, Luhring
Augustine, New York and Galerie Barbara
Weiss, Berlin

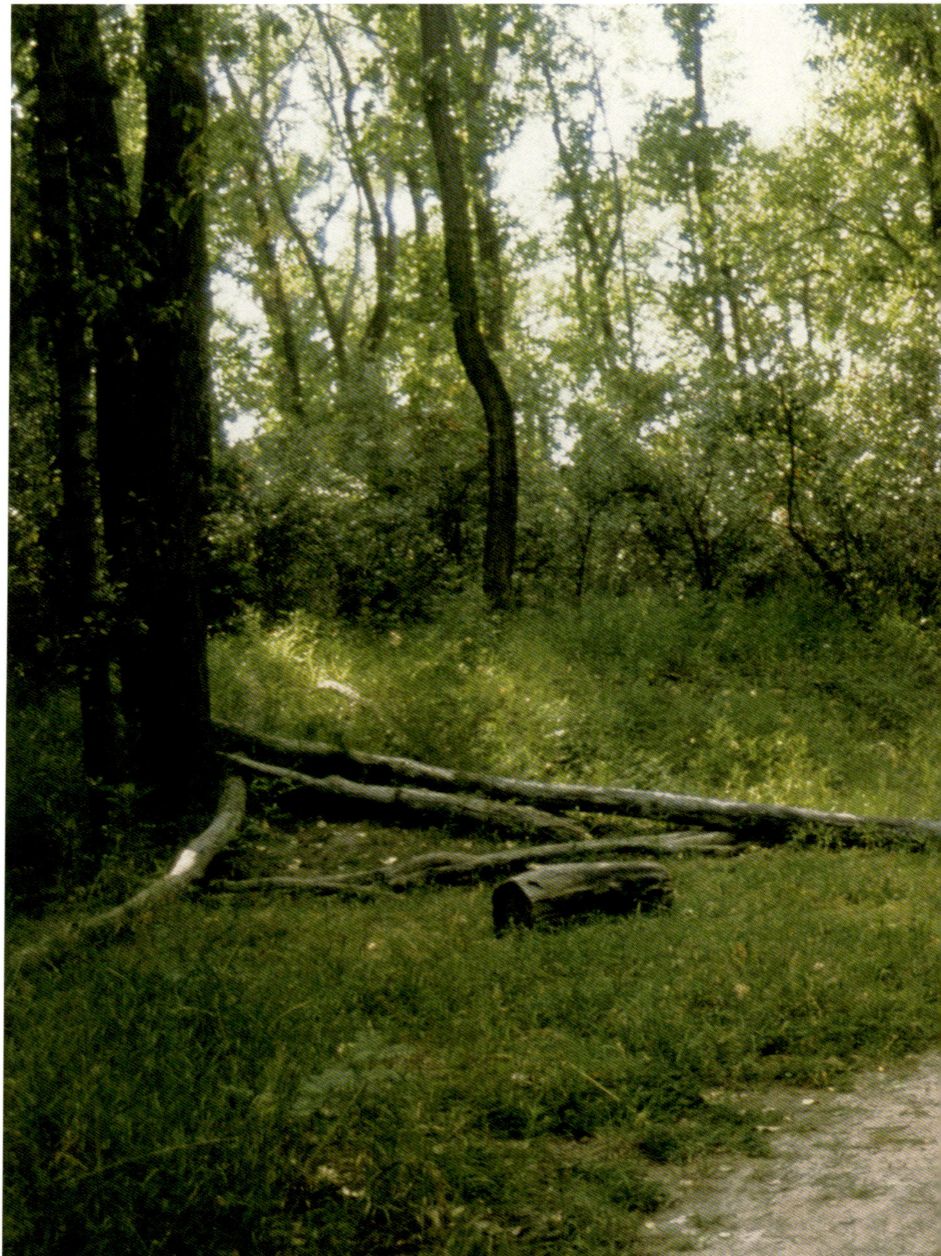

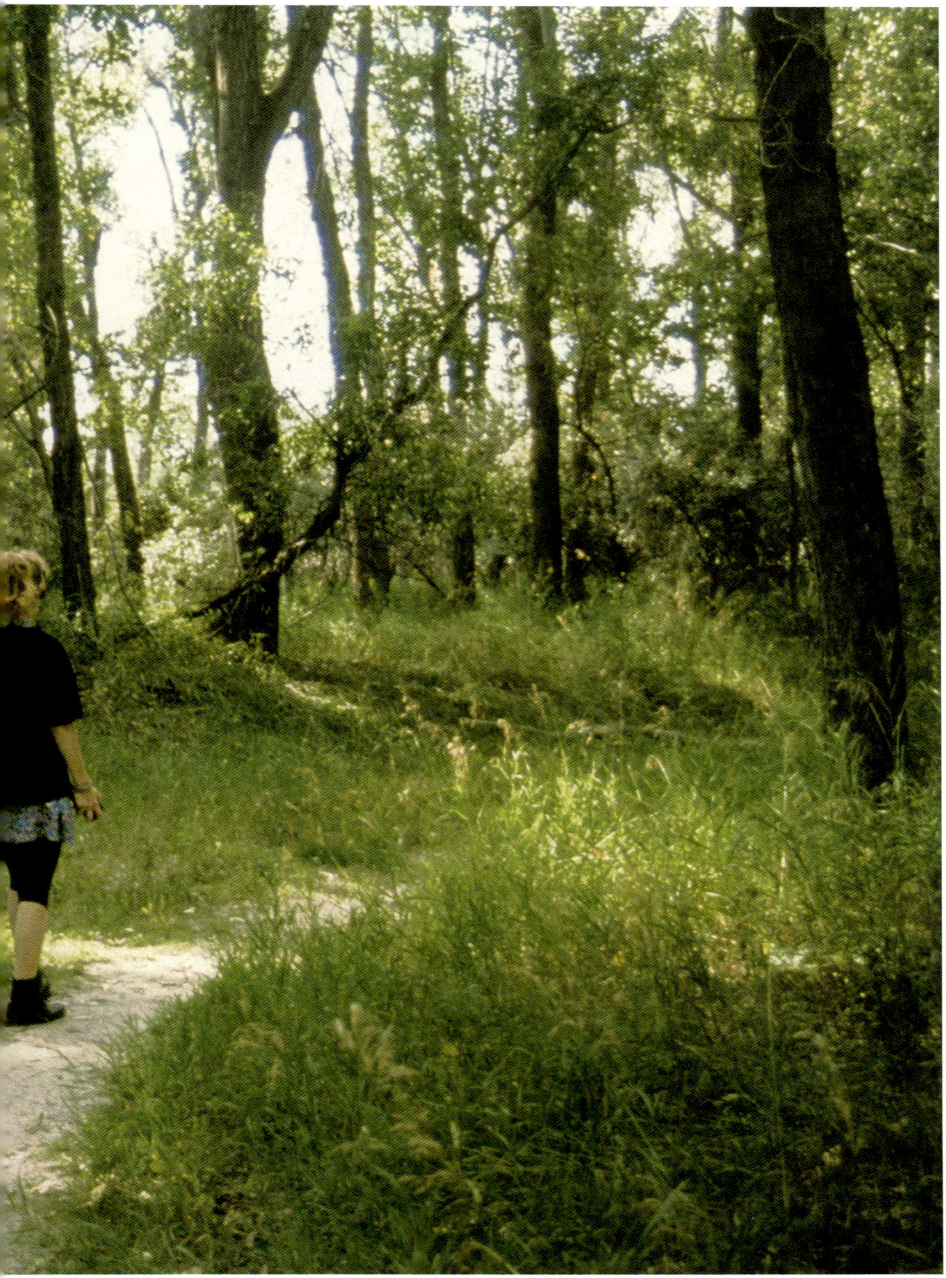

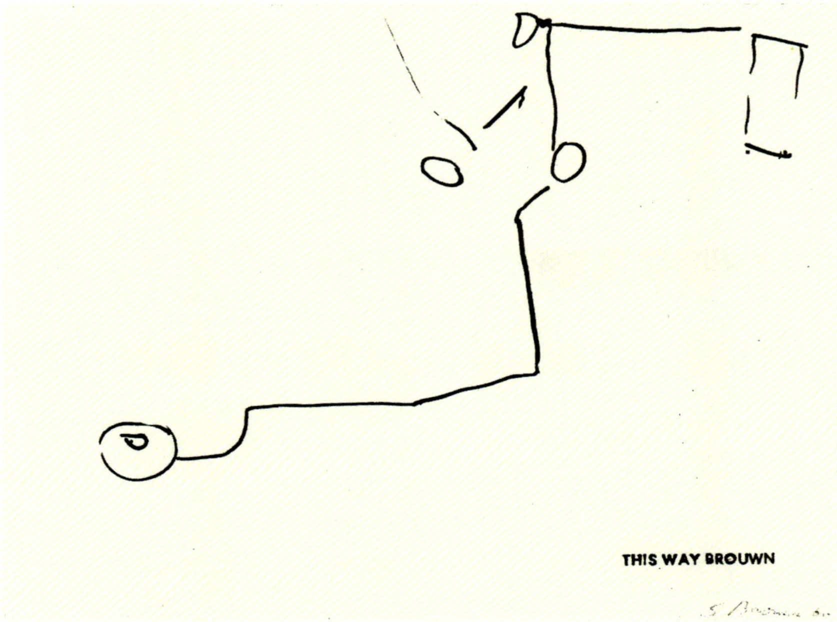

15. Stanley Brouwn,
This Way Brouwn, 1960,
felt-tipped pen and pencil on paper,
21 × 29.7cm

Image courtesy of the artist

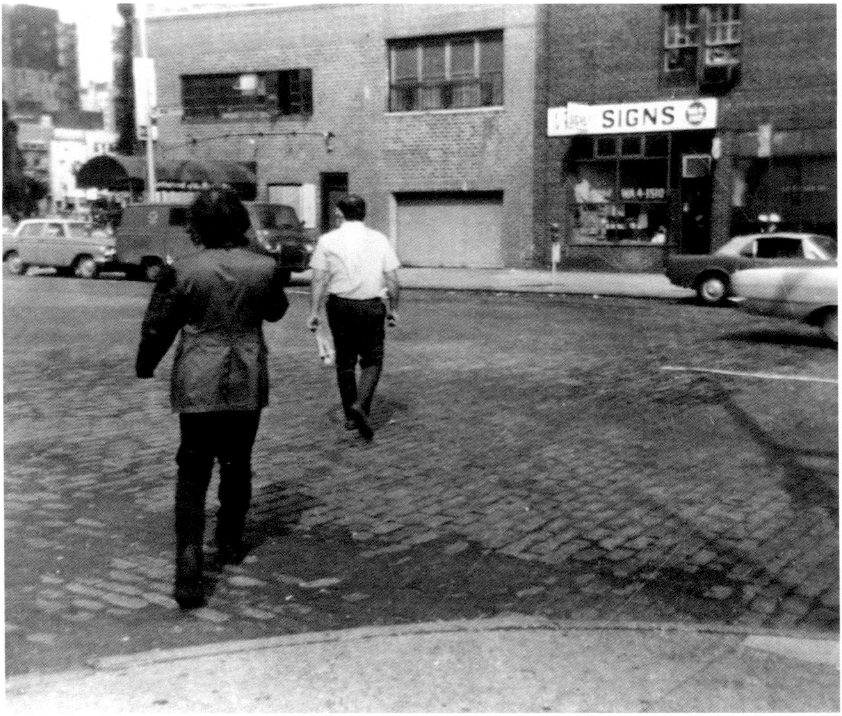

16—17. Vito Acconci,
Following Piece, 1969,
gelatin silver print,
8 × 8cm each, documentation of the
performance made on occasion of the
'Street Works IV' Program, organised
by the Architectural League,
New York, 3—25 October 1969

FOLLOWING PIECE
'Street Works IV', Architectural League of NY; Oct 3-25,1969; NYC, various locations.
Activity (walking); New York, NY, various locations; 23 days, varying times each day

Once a day, wherever I happen to be, I pick out, at random, a person walking in the street.

Each day I follow a different person; I keep following until that person disappears into a private place (home, office, etc.) where I can no longer follow.

(The terms of the exhibition, 'Street Works IV', were: to do a piece, sometime during the month, that had as its subject matter a street in New York City. FOLLOWING PIECE, potentially, could use all the time allotted and all the space available: I might be following people all day long, everyday, throughout all the streets in the city. In actuality, episodes of following ranged from 2 or 3 minutes - when someone got into a car and I couldn't grab a taxi fast enough, I couldn't follow - to 7 or 8 hours - when a person went to a restaurant, a movie...)

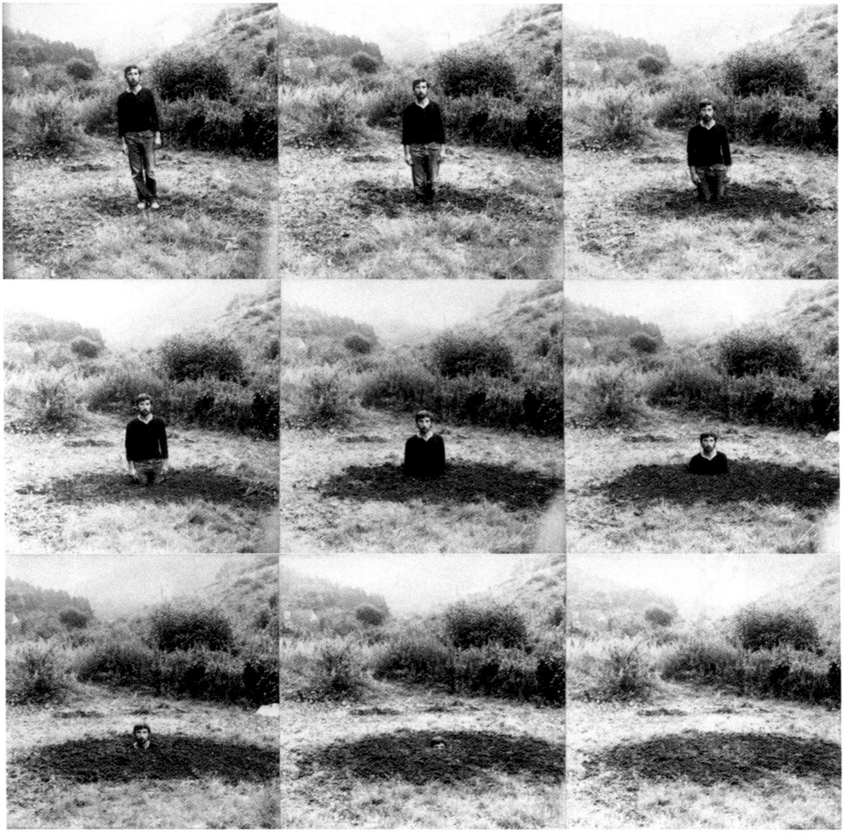

18. Keith Arnatt,
Self Burial (In Nine Stages), 1969,
nine photographs mounted on board,
overall dimensions 22.9 × 205.7cm

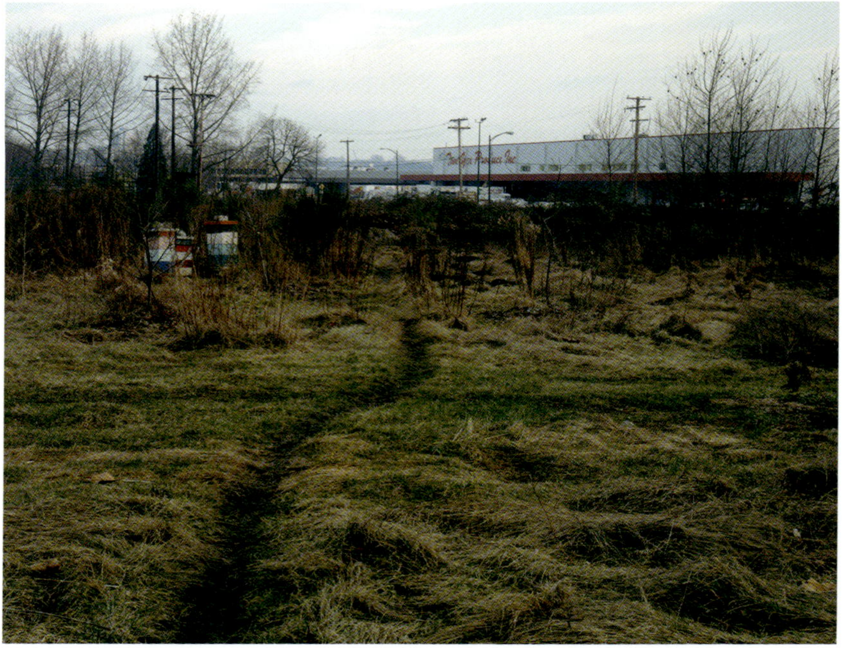

19. Jeff Wall,
The Crooked Path, 1991,
Cibachrome transparency in lightbox,
documentary photograph, 119 × 149cm

project — thousands of visitors apparently showed up on the exhibition's opening night, waiting to be let into the gallery to see *nothing at all* — was an especially forceful example of the mystique of the void then about to sweep the international art world.[64] In Klein's native France the theatrical collusion of absurd comedy, mechanical repetition (or reproduction) and craftily staged withdrawal would eventually culminate in the well-publicised *succès de scandale* of the artist collective BMPT. The artists were Daniel Buren, Olivier Mosset, Michel Parmentier and Niele Toroni, who, in 1967, pulled out of their very first group exhibition under a great deal of public attention, after having spent a full day robotically making paintings in their own signature, mechanically depersonalised styles. Buren produced his 8.7-centimetre-wide vertical stripes, Mosset his small black circles centred on blank canvases, Parmentier his sprayed horizontal bands and Toroni his regular pattern of imprints made with a no. 50 brush at 30-centimetre intervals; these quasi-machine traces not unlike the simple, straight or circular lines walked or drawn by Richard Long in his early earth works of around the same time. (Long's and BMPT's interest in the anaemic aesthetic of the trace — the less artful the better — attests to a shared fascination with the business of depersonalisation.) Half a year later, the aforementioned quartet installed their paintings (one by each artist) above the stage in the lecture hall of the Musée des Art Décoratifs in Paris:

After an hour in which nothing happened, they passed out a paper to the bemused and fidgeting audience, telling them that 'obviously this is only a matter of looking at the paintings of Buren, Mosset, Parmentier and Toroni'. Marcel Duchamp (the greatest escape artist of them all), who was present, remarked, 'What a frustrating happening: one couldn't have done it better!'[65]

And this all happened, incidentally, around the same time that Guy Debord prophesied, in *The Society of the Spectacle*, that 'art's vanguard is its own disappearance'.[66]

Among the more direct or more earnest references to the 'Eastern' aesthetic of avoidance and nothingness that determined much of the context out of which some of Richard Long's work arose, we should also mention Nam June Paik's *Zen for Film* from 1964 — a cinematographic variation on Cage's silence (Cage and Paik were frequent collaborators in the Fluxus/happening scene of the early 1960s). *Zen for Film* consists of an endless loop of unexposed film running through a projector, with the resulting projected image showing a surface illuminated by a bright light, occasionally altered by the appearance of scratches and dust particles in the surface of the damaged film material. As Heike Helfert has noted, 'as an analogy to John Cage, who included silence as a non-sound in his music, Paik uses the emptiness of the image for his art. This is a film which depicts only itself and its own material qualities, and which, as an "anti-film", is meant to encourage viewers to oppose the flood of images from outside with one's own interior images.'[67] The now largely forgotten North American artist Christine Kozlov (like Long, born in 1945), who co-founded the Museum of Normal Art with Joseph Kosuth in 1967, showed a very similar work, *Transparent Film #2* (1967), during the opening exhibition of that short-lived artist initiative. The work consisted of an 'empty' or blank 16mm film spool, and in a sense presaged Kozlov's own gradual disappearance from view within the narrow confines of the Conceptual and post-Conceptual art world.[68] Along with Lee Lozano, Charlotte Posenenske, Tehching Hsieh and, above all, Bas Jan Ader, Kozlov was one of a number of artists who actively sought out polemical, existential extremes. One of Lozano's programmatic diary entries from 1969, written one year before embarking on her famous *Dropout Piece*, commands us to always

'Seek the Extremes' of withdrawal, erasure and loss; in Ader's hyperbolic case, this resounds in the tragic enactment of the art of disappearance in his own premature death — encountered, one might say, during 'a line made by sailing' across the Atlantic.[69] The shadow of death, or thanatos, that hovers over these various exercises in escapology reveals the traumatic flip side of all heroic attempts to dissolve art into life. Similarly, subtle echoes of mourning and melancholia certainly, and inevitably, haunt *A Line Made by Walking* — if only because a black-and-white photograph of a gesture long forgotten, of a shadowy trace long gone, of an artwork long dead, is all that remains: the 'spectral evidence' of a temporary scar drawn across a field of grass, England, 1967.[70] And so the very transience of *A Line Made by Walking*, so emblematic of the epoch's fascination with various forms of disappearance, diffusion and dissolution — that which, in Robert Smithson's terminology, is simply named 'entropy' — seems to serve here as a symbol for the transience of all living things proper, for the fateful brittleness of all art rooted (if only as a critique of commodification) in the practice of everyday life, as well as, much less morbidly, for the irreducible 'absence' that is at the heart of all presence.

This brief invocation of the dialectic of absence and presence (in the work of Richard Long as in that of so many of his travelling companions) relates back to the groundbreaking philosophical work of Jacques Derrida, whose triptych *Speech and Phenomena*, *Of Grammatology* and *Writing and Difference* was also published in 1967 (afterwards named the philosopher's *annus mirabilis* because of the amplitude of the shockwaves these three books in particular would send through the world of human sciences). If the spirit of Derrida's *Of Grammatology* could be condensed to a variation upon Descartes's wisecrack, 'I speak therefore I am present, I write therefore I must be absent', then Long's *A Line Made by Walking* seems to have replaced the speaking/writing dyad with that of the actual walk and the photographic record of its physical effects and results (walking implies 'presence', photography implies 'absence'). And, of course, *A Line Made by Walking* does operate as a writing of sorts, as a line 'written' in the grass — a fact that is further compounded by photography's etymological roots in the history of writing ('writing with light'). A black-and-white photograph of a line made by walking then appears as 'writing of writing' — a doubled-up absence, so to speak. Like Foucault's *The Order of Things*, Derrida's early works belong to the same cultural 'history of disappearance' that Long's walks are such an integral part of, and his damning critique of the Western philosophical tradition as a 'metaphysics of presence' coincides with various similar critiques of 'presence' (of the artist's signature, for instance, or of the artist's authority in the demonstration of skill) in so much of the art made at the time.

An Imprint of Indifference

Any consideration of the role of (self-)effacement and evaporation in the work of Richard Long and his contemporaries, and in *A Line Made by Walking* in particular, must conclude by returning to the following question: *where* is the work of art in *A Line Made by Walking*, and where is its essence or substance? Does it lie in the walking or in its record? Part of the answer to this question (if it is no longer to be found in Surrey) must lie in the photograph of the work, as well as in the part played by photography in much art of the late 1960s.

Just like Joseph Kosuth's *One and Three Chairs* from 1965 (an installation consisting of a chair, a photograph of a chair, and a typewritten dictionary definition of a chair), Dan Graham's *Homes for America* from 1966—67 (a photo-essay first published in *Arts Magazine* in 1966) and Robert Barry's *Closed Gallery*

Piece from 1969, *A Line Made by Walking* has entered Conceptual art folklore — a rumour in that it is so much easier talked about than actually 'seen' — because of the confusion it wilfully inspires: we may have heard or read somewhere that the work is an action, event or performance — a time-bound gesture with only fleeting 'sculptural' consequences: the contours of a line, a shimmering Barnett Newman-like 'zip'. But it is also a *photograph*, and not just instrumentally or perfunctorily so — not merely a documentary, quasi-journalistic registration of Long's short-lived intervention in the natural environment. *A Line Made by Walking* is a photograph *too*, although made with — and this is probably much more significant than it may then have appeared — a very primitive camera. It is an emblematic instance of photography as either Conceptual art per se or crucially implicated in Conceptual art practice: a textbook example of the pivotal role assumed by photography, not just in Long's work or in the creation of this work in particular, but in the early Conceptual art and Land art movements more generally. For it is sufficiently clear that Conceptual, 'non-objective' art as such would probably have been unthinkable without the radical departures afforded by the critical reconsideration of photography as a tool for art-making. As Jeff Wall has noted in an influential essay devoted to the subject, 'Marks of Indifference: Aspects of Photography in, or as, Conceptual Art' (1995), which also includes a reflection on Richard Long's work in photography, 'many of Conceptual art's essential achievements were either created in the form of photographs or were otherwise mediated by them'.[71] Indeed, of the 'proletarian' photography in Long's *A Line Made by Walking* in particular, Wall says it is typical of a moment in art characterised by what he calls:

the introversion, or subjectivisation, of reportage as manifested in two important directions. First, it brought photography in a new relationship with the problematic of the staged, or posed, picture, through new concepts of performance. Second, the inscription of photography into a nexus of experimental practices led to a direct but distantiated and parodic relationship with the art-concept of photojournalism.[72]

A Line Made by Walking is more inclined towards the first direction than towards the second, and therefore in it:

the picture is presented as the subsidiary form of an act, as 'photo-documentation'. It has become that, however, by means of a new kind of photographic mise en scène. *That is, it exists and is legitimated as continuous with the project of reportage by moving in precisely the opposite direction, toward a completely designed pictorial method, an introverted masquerade that plays games with the inherited aesthetic proclivities of art-photography-as-reportage.* [...] *This integration or fusion of reportage and performance, its manneristic introversion, can be seen as an implicitly parodic critique of the concepts of art-photography.*[73]

Perhaps *A Line Made by Walking*, in its relative crudeness, also acts as a prophetic parody — though this is probably too strong a term, especially for a work conceived and executed so intuitively, almost instinctively — of the subsequent professionalisation of all manner of 'reportage' in art photography.

Like many artists of his generation, Long experienced a minor revelation when he first saw the artist's books by Ed Ruscha that did so much to revolutionise both the concept of the artist's book (which one might say Ruscha even 'invented', certainly in its present guise; his *Thirtyfour Parking Lots*, which consists of 34 black-and-white aerial photographs, taken at the artist's instruction by Art Alanis, of parking lots in and around the city of Los Angeles, was published in 1967) as well as the use of photography in contemporary art.[74] These books effectively brought about the 'liberation' of photography from the oppressive 'compulsion' to emulate the pictorial idioms and idiosyncrasies of fine art, conversely leading artists to mimic the amateur, 'anti-art' look of mundane, vernacular (or 'use') photography instead.

Without a doubt, long before Ruscha, photography had established itself as a fine art — one that was nonetheless still considered clearly distinct from the field of visual or pictorial art proper, to which it was deemed inferior (largely for genealogical reasons of the latter's seniority, but also for economic reasons of market valuation). The early Soviet-Russian experiment in art and Walter Benjamin's seminal essay 'The Work of Art in the Age of Mechanical Reproduction' (1935), along with widely read texts by Roland Barthes and Susan Sontag, had contributed significantly to photography's gradual artistic ennoblement, but even a cursory glance at both the art history of the early post-War period and its complement in the field of fine arts photography reveals to what extent the latter merely existed alongside the 'higher' realm of painting and sculpture, with very little crossover activity being initiated from either side of this invisible divide. Things started to change dramatically in the 1960s, however, as more and more artists sought to leave behind the constraints of the studio space and its traditional, object-driven modes of production, to venture out into the (real) world to realise transitory works whose temporary materialisation could often only be captured by way of photographic documentation or, far more rarely, with 8mm film. The turn towards photography, even if initially only as a second-hand medium of registration and memorialisation, was thus deeply implicated in the larger trend towards the dematerialisation of the art object and the critiques of production and productivism which buttressed this trend.

Much of the interest in photography at the time was therefore pragmatist as well as resolutely 'ideological' — the result of Conceptual art's alignment with all things non- or anti-art. With regard to the first virtue, as Long himself remarked in conversation, photography enabled him to make art everywhere (as allowed by situational, post-studio practice), and to show people around the world what he 'did' — quite a few early photographic works were actually developed at the various chemists he would come across during his travels.[75] On one such trip, to New York in 1969, where he spent some time before travelling onwards to Ithaca to participate in the landmark 'Earth Art' exhibition at Cornell University's Andrew Dickson White Museum, Long in fact met a gallerist in a bar who, upon seeing the photographs Long was taking around with him in a simple cigar box, invited him to show at his gallery.[76] The subsequent realisation by Long that photographs could be works of art of their own eventually landed the 23-year-old artist his first solo exhibition in the United States, held at the John Gibson Gallery in SoHo in the early spring of 1969.

The grainy, emphatically amateur quality of many photographs of works of art (or of many photographs *as* works of art) that we now regard as the canonical, iconic nodes in the history of Conceptual art is clearly related to the defiant identification with 'amateur' culture (as opposed to the perceived evils of professional, managerial culture) which characterised so much cultural activity throughout the 1960s. (How easily this quality has been fetishised, in the meantime, as a true marker of authenticity and radicalism, to become a style — or form — rather than an attitude!) Indeed, one important aspect of the radically new approach to photography initiated by the likes of Ed Ruscha and Dan Graham was its critique of skill and of the emphasis, in older and more established traditions of 'art photography', on the mastery of form and technique as a way of securing photography's inclusion in the pantheon of high art. Although 'de-skilling', whether as an actual artistic fact or as a mere rhetorical claim, had been integral to twentieth-century avant-gardism (it had been *the* critical element of art 'production' in Duchamp's readymade in particular), it is really only with the advent of Conceptual art that the notion acquired a programmatic, quasi-political dimension, mobilised more specifically to challenge the hierarchical structures of the art world, which were thought to reflect the hierarchical structures of the world at large. This idea of deskilling as a radical political gesture is essentially what motivated Joseph Beuys's polemical contention that everyone *is*, or that everyone *should be* an artist — and not just for fifteen minutes. As Jeff Wall recounts in 'Marks of Indifference':

the utopian project of rediscovering the roots of creativity in a spontaneity and intersubjectivity freed from all specialisation and spectacularised expertise combined with the actual profusion of light consumer technologies to legitimate a widespread 'de-skilling' and 're-skilling' of art and art education. [...] *it was no longer necessary to separate oneself from the people through the acquisition of skills and sensibilities rooted in craft-guild exclusivity and secrecy; in fact it was absolutely necessary not to do so, but rather to animate with radical imagination those common techniques and abilities made available by modernity itself. First among these was photography.*[77]

The photographic medium was subjected to 'a full-scale immersion in the logic of reductivism' — the reduction, that is, to what Wall calls the 'anaesthetic, the look of non-art, the condition of no-art and the loss of the visual'. In other words, 'the essential reduction came on the level of skill', leading to the widespread adoption, around 1966, of what

Wall calls 'the mimesis of amateurism'.[78] In his essay, Wall goes on to situate this event within the larger historical context of photographic technology, at the moment when Nikon and Polaroid revolutionised Kodak's classical 'Eastman era' of amateur photography. The mimesis of amateurism thus:

takes place at the threshold of a new technological situation, one in which the image-producing capacity of the average citizen was about to make a quantum leap. It is thus, historically speaking, really the last moment of 'amateur photography' as such, as a social category established and maintained by custom and technique. Conceptualism turns toward the past just as the past darts by into the future; it elegises something at the same instant that it points toward the glimmering actualisation of avant-garde utopianism through technological progress.[79]

It is worth quoting Wall's essay at length here for more than one reason, as Long's and Wall's artistic trajectories also intersect at a lesser-known early stage in the latter's career. Some seven years before producing the first large-scale, backlit transparencies for which he became known, Wall was already quite active in the burgeoning Conceptual art scene of his hometown Vancouver, an important hub in Lucy Lippard's *Six Years* — Lippard had in fact organised one of her first landmark Conceptual art exhibitions ('955,000', 1970) in Vancouver. *Landscape Manual* (1970), one of Wall's earliest preserved works (made when he was 23, one year older than Long when he made *A Line Made by Walking*) was an extended Conceptual performance made during long, seemingly aimless drives through a suburban wasteland of intersections, dead zones and post-industrial desolation, with Wall intermittently snapping away — in the mimetic-amateurist manner theorised in his essay from 1995 — at the underwhelming surrounds, the 'defeatured landscape'.[80] This Situationist-inflected *dérive* was then documented in a brochure made up of black-and-white photographs and typewritten commentary. Wall's *Landscape Manual* thus belongs to an expanding body of quasi-documentary art practices influenced by Ed Ruscha and Robert Smithson and marked, in essence, by indifference.

In Richard Long's photograph of *A Line Made by Walking*, the aforementioned elegiac quality is especially palpable, given that its object is itself a thing of the past impossible to sustain in the present, let alone permanently imprint on the future — a path of trampled-upon grass in a field somewhere outside London that most probably isn't there anymore. The photograph is all that is left of it, but not quite in the same detached, foppish way that is characteristic of, for example, Ruscha's pictures of the Sunset Strip or Smithson's snapshots of the monuments of Passaic, New Jersey. The difference, once again, seems related to distinctive cultural approaches to (natural versus urban) landscape. Perhaps Yves Klein's 'leap into the void' from 1960 is a better point of reference for *A Line Made by Walking*. Both works trace a singular gesture, which the photograph semi-authoritatively preserves in its mild glow of historical authenticity. It stakes an auratic claim of testimonial uniqueness in the notoriously myth-prone, event-centred methodology of body or performance art — an authenticity made more convincing through its amateur quality, made more gripping because of its being black and white. The crucial difference is, of course, that Klein never leapt into the void — the whole thing (the photograph, that is) is a ruse, a fiction, an early exercise in the mendacious art of photo-collage. Whereas Richard Long really *did* walk up and down a field in Surrey in 1967. Didn't he?

Post Scriptum: A Trip Made by Driving

For I do not understand, and I never shall understand, how it can be a pleasure to hurtle past all the images and objects which our beautiful earth displays, as if one had gone mad and had to accelerate for fear of misery and despair.
— Robert Walser, 'The Walk'[81]

When I visited Richard Long at his house, a former village school in the countryside just outside Bristol, in January 2009, to ask him a couple of questions about *A Line Made by Walking*, one such question concerned the exact location of the field of grass where this line had first been walked. Long admitted to not exactly remembering. This was rather disappointing, as I had harboured hopes of actually venturing out to find the field in question — assuming, of course, that it still existed — to perhaps walk a line myself, and make a photograph of 'my' line made by walking.

I then asked him whether he was aware of the existence of any re-enactments of the work, what with re-enactments being a major creative industry in the contemporary art world today. I had actually come across one such re-enactment myself — a certain Rupert White from Cornwall effectively redrew Long's original line in 2007, naming it *A Line Made by Walking (Landfill)*, executed on a site used for landfill. Long answered me that he himself had re-enacted the piece once for a BBC documentary sometime in the early 1980s. I didn't ask him where this second *Line Made by Walking* had been made (and I didn't mention Rupert White's Line either), although I was surprised to hear Long admit to having enjoyed the idea, at least, of bringing the work back to life again, in another time, at another place. This begged the question as to whether an artwork such as this can ever be remade, or how much of it can ever be remade — a question that is perhaps all the more pressing for those works of art that consist of the simplest, most quotidian and forgettable of gestures. Such inscriptions of thought as Long's, materially grounded in earth, are more easily conjured, it seems, in writing.

Driving me back to Bristol to catch my early evening train, Long rather dryly remarked upon the supreme irony of being driven around the countryside by a famous walking artist. In the meantime, Somerset's darkening surrounds flitted by, and the memory of something I had read not long ago came creeping back:

We make a mistake, says Seamus Heaney, if, driving down a road between wind and water, overwhelmed by what we see, we assume we will see 'it' better if we stop the car. It is there in the passage.[82]

1
Friedrich Nietzsche, *Ecce Homo* (trans. R.J. Hollingdale), Harmondsworth: Penguin Books, 1979, p.54.

2
Richard Cork in conversation with the artist, in Richard Long, *Walking in Circles*, London: Thames & Hudson, 1991, p.249.

3
British, Los Angeles-based author Geoff Nicholson playfully lists some thirty-plus 'synonyms' for walking in *The Lost Art of Walking: The History, Science, Philosophy, and Literature of Pedestrianism*, London and New York: Riverhead, 2008.

4
Robert Walser, 'The Walk', *Selected Stories* (trans. Christopher Middleton), New York: Farrar, Strauss and Giroux, 1982, p.53.

5
A Line Made by Walking also literally signalled the advent of the post-Duchampian age in that it was made a year before Duchamp's death in 1968, and two years before the unveiling of *Étant donnés* (1946—66) at the Philadelphia Museum of Art, the work that catapulted Duchamp back into the limelight of art-historical polemics.

6
Long has often quoted Carl Andre's work in sculpture as an important reference point for his work, if only for the power of his linear floor sculptures, the echoes of which resound throughout Long's own practice. Long met Andre for the first time at Konrad Fischer's gallery in Düsseldorf in 1968, on the occasion of *Prospekt 68*, organised by Hans Strelow and Fischer at the Kunsthalle Düsseldorf. An untitled work by Andre shown at Paula Cooper Gallery in New York in 1969 is listed as a 'portrait of Richard Long' by Lucy R. Lippard in *Six Years: The Dematerialization of the Art Object from 1966 to 1972*, New York: Praeger, 1973, p.100.

7
The term 'Arte Povera' was first coined by Italian art critic Germano Celant as part of the title of an exhibition he curated at Galleria La Bertesca in Genoa in the fall of 1967. Long's trajectory as an artist intersected with the history of Arte Povera on numerous occasions, the earliest instance being an experimental arts festival organised in the historic port of Amalfi in October 1968, titled 'Arte Povera + azioni povere', with Long's work clearly belonging to the latter category of 'poor actions'. His contribution to the festival consisted of two pieces, one being a performance during which the artist, wearing a St. Martin's School of Art sweater, shook the hands of some twenty-odd unsuspecting passers-by. The photographs of the performance are rather unusual in that they actually depict the artist 'at work'. In later years, Long himself would hardly ever show up in his own work. The second work done in Amalfi, a white wooden plank hung from one of the cliffs that jut out of the port's craggy hinterland, reflected Long's continued interest in the question of distancing and perspective, which had also informed the perspectival appearance (in the photograph) of *A Line Made by Walking* and works such as *England 1968* (1968). This concern was equally present in the work of Land art colleagues such as Jan Dibbets.

8
In this context, Long has likened his work to music, saying 'like a piece of music, there can exist different versions of the same work'. Conversation with the artist, January 2009.

9
See Theodor W. Adorno, 'Cultural Criticism and Society', *Prisms* (trans. Samuel and Shierry Weber), Cambridge, MA and London: The MIT Press, 1967, p.34.

10
During the 'Second Gutai Exhibition', organised in Osaka in 1956, Akira Kanayama created a work simply titled *Footsteps*, consisting of a 1,500-metre-long path or line of white vinyl marked with footsteps wending through the exhibition to simply stop at a tree.

11
See David Kynaston, *Austerity Britain: 1945—1951*, London: Walker & Company, 2008.

12
In the same conversation I had with Long in January 2009, he commented that 'you cannot walk a straight line in the city — therefore I am not an urban artist'. In many ways, Long is not just a rural artist but also a *local* artist, whose work remains intimately connected — and self-consciously so — with his living environment in the southwest of England. Long's mud circles, for instance, have been made using mud from the River Avon, near Bristol.

13
Quoted in Rebecca Solnit, *Wanderlust: A History of Walking*, London and New York: Verso, 2002, p.164. The original source is Raphael Samuel, *Theatres of Memory*, London and New York: Verso, 1996, p.297. Samuel continues: '"freedom to roam" was a left-wing campaigning issue. [...] Hiking had a particular appeal to working-class Bohemians, as a mainly intellectual alternative to dance halls, and one that cost no money.'

14
Long was on a vocational course run by Frank Martin, taught by Peter Atkins. Anthony Caro was one of the dominant figures in the British art world at the time — a position of influence that was not always greatly appreciated, as is attested to by the radical anti-materiality of so much of the work produced by his students at the time. Long's relationship with the gospel of Greenbergian modernism, which Caro's work seemed to represent back then, was primarily one of indifference. This, too, set him apart from some of his contemporaries, who took a more active, impassioned part in the polemic. John Latham, also a lecturer at St. Martin's School of Art at the time — though he did leave the school before Long's arrival — rather literally acted out this widespread anti-Greenbergian sentiment (at least in the Atlantic art context) in a notorious performance remembered in his obituary published in *The Guardian* on 7 January 2006: 'Back in the 1960s he had invited his students to join him in a feast where the main course was to be Clement Greenberg's book *Art and Culture*, a volume of art theory. This, they chewed up and spat out for Latham to bottle, distil, decant into a phial and put into a leather case to be

displayed as a work entitled *Spit and Chew: Art and Culture* and now owned, but rarely displayed, by the Museum of Modern Art in New York.' See http://www.guardian.co.uk/news/2006/jan/07/guardianobituaries.artsobituaries (last accessed on 17 December 2009).

15
The key texts here are *A Philosophical Enquiry into the Origin of Our Ideas of the Sublime and Beautiful*, written by Edmund Burke in 1757, and Kant's *Observations on the Feeling of the Beautiful and Sublime*, published in 1764.

16
Only very few women figure in this intellectual history, even though walking would eventually be named a prototypical 'country lady's amusement', according to Dorothy Wordsworth in a letter from 1792, quoted in R. Solnit, *Wanderlust*, *op. cit.*, p.97. The original source is *Letters of William and Dorothy Wordsworth: Vol. I, The Early Years, 1787—1805* (ed. Ernest de Selincourt), Oxford: Clarendon Press, 1967, p.84.

17
Jean-Jacques Rousseau, *The Confessions* (trans. J.M. Cohen), Harmondsworth: Penguin Books, 1954, p.382. Solnit paraphrases this fragment when she writes: 'I suspect that the mind, like the feet, works at about three miles an hour.' R. Solnit, *Wanderlust, op. cit.*, p.10.

18
According to Solnit, however, Kant's walking habits were informed more by dietary concerns and health considerations than by an actual passion for walking for walking's sake: 'frail Immanuel Kant took a daily walk around Königsberg after dinner — but it was merely for exercise, because he did his thinking sitting by the stove and staring at the church tower out the window'. R. Solnit, *Wanderlust*, *op. cit.*, p.16.

19
Ibid., quoting from *Selected Letters of Friedrich Nietzsche* (ed. Oscar Levy, trans. Anthony M. Ludovici), New York: Doubleday, 1921, p.23. Nietzsche himself — the first real philosopher of *movement* and *mobility*, famously describing 'truth as a mobile army of metaphors, metonyms and anthropomorphisms' — is one of the principal walkers of nineteenth-century history, whether in the mountains surrounding his summer retreat in the Swiss village of Sils-Maria, in the streets of Turin or in the cities on the French Riviera. The little Riviera village of Eze has an actual trail named Le Chemin de Nietzsche. Schopenhauer was also a great devotee of Kant, and, following the latter's example, lived according to a strict routine that included a daily two-hour walk through his hometown of Frankfurt am Main.

20
Ibid., p.23. Solnit also references a similar experience of walking as a physical trigger for imagining the world outside, this time lived by the high-ranking Nazi architect Albert Speer, who 'traversed the world in his imagination while pacing back and forth in his prison yard'. Speer laid out a path in the garden he had created inside the yard, and after using it for mere daily exercise it became the blank canvas

onto which he projected his fantasies of freely walking around the world outside the Spandau prison gates — first from Berlin to Heidelberg, but soon after embarking on a trip around the world (which he mapped out with the help of a steady stream of maps, guidebooks and atlases). On the day of his release in 1966, after nineteen years in prison, he had apparently arrived in Guadalajara, Mexico. *Ibid.*, p.76.

21
Ibid., p.27.

22
Ibid., p.5.

23
Ibid., p.29.

24
Michel de Certeau, *The Practice of Everyday Life* (trans. Steven Rendall), Berkeley: University of California Press, 1984, pp.97—98. De Certeau's interweaving of walking and talking could be read as a comment upon the triangulation of talking, walking and writing (if only 'with light', as in 'photo-graphy'), which I will return to later, when discussing Jacques Derrida's contribution to the development of a theory of disappearance at the exact time as Long's participation in the practice of disappearance is taking shape.

25
R. Solnit, *Wanderlust*, *op. cit.*, p.83.

26
Terry Eagleton, *The Ideology of the Aesthetic*, Oxford: Blackwell, 1991, p.13.

27
R. Solnit, *Wanderlust*, *op. cit.*, p.83. See also, on p.109: 'to walk in the gracious and expensive confines of the [French] garden was to associate walking, nature, the leisure classes, and the established order that secured that leisure. To walk in the world was to link walking with a nature aligned instead with the poor and whatever radicalism would defend their rights and interests.'

28
Ibid., p.93. On the notion of 'pilgrimage' as an early precursor of present-day tourism and on the role played by walking in this experience specifically, it is worth mentioning here that one of modern art's defining epic walks was undertaken by Constantin Brancusi in the early 1920s to reach the undisputed world capital of art at the time, Paris. Brancusi consciously (and not uncynically) emphasised the pseudo-religious nature of his undertaking, pandering to the orientalist tastes of his newly found Parisian public by regularly dressing up in shaman-like 'Eastern' garb. On a related pseudo-religious note, the notion of travel as 'an end in itself' is an almost literal foreshadowing of the popular Taoist wisdom that 'the journey itself is the reward'; I will be returning to the impact of Zen imagery upon much art of 1960s and 70s later in this book.

29
Long has highlighted the importance of the early Mail art networks to his practice at the time. New York Conceptual art impresario Seth Siegelaub worked together with him on at least one 'immaterial' exhibition project, 'July-August-September, 1969', which took place in eleven different locations all over the world. Long's project took place in his hometown of Bristol, Robert Smithson's in the far-flung Yucatan, Lawrence Weiner's at Niagara Falls, etc. Conversation with the artist, January 2009.

30
Samuel J. Wagstaff, Jr, 'Talking with Tony Smith', *Artforum*, vol.5, no.4, December 1966, pp.21—23.

31
The reference here is to the work of French theorists Gilles Deleuze and Félix Guattari, whose *A Thousand Plateaus* in particular has been widely influential since its publication in 1980. In their introductory chapter on the rhizome, Deleuze and Guattari state that 'there are no points or positions in a rhizome ... *there are only lines*' (the author's emphasis). Furthermore, the rhizome — technically a thick horizontal underground stem of plants — is also 'a map and not a tracing', for 'what distinguishes the map from the tracing is that it is entirely oriented toward an experimentation in contact with the real'. A lasting motif in Long's work, as well as in that of many of his early travelling companions such as Art & Language, Douglas Huebler and Dennis Oppenheim, the map 'is open and connectable in all of its dimensions. [...] The map has to do with performance, whereas the tracing always involves an alleged "competence".' G. Deleuze and F. Guattari, *A Thousand Plateaus* (trans. Brian Massumi), London: The Athlone Press, 1988, pp.8—13.

32
Francis Alÿs, one of contemporary art's better-known walkers, has occasionally referenced Richard Long in his work, whether critically (in his decision to politicise walking, or tentatively de-romanticise the legacy of Land art in works such as *When Faith Moves Mountains* [2002], in which 500 volunteers were mobilised to move a sand dune outside Lima, Peru using only shovels) or sympathetically (in *Pebble Walk* [1999], a subdued homage to Long consisting of no more than a seventy-minute walk through Hyde Park after which Alÿs counted the pebbles that got stuck in his shoes).

33
'Urban walking has always been a shadier business, easily turning into soliciting, cruising, promenading, shopping, rioting, protesting, skulking, loitering and other activities that, however enjoyable, hardly have the high moral tone of nature appreciation.' R. Solnit, *Wanderlust*, *op. cit.*, p.173.

34
Guy Debord, 'Théorie de la dérive', *Internationale Situationniste* #2, 1958. Reprinted in Ken Knabb (ed.), *Situationist Anthology*, London: Bureau of Public Secrets, 2007, as well as online at http://www.bopsecrets.org/SI/2.derive.htm (last accessed on 14 December 2009). On a more practical note, Debord goes on to warn that 'the average duration of a *dérive* is one day, considered as the time between two periods of sleep. The starting and ending times have no necessary relation to the solar day, but it should be noted that the last hours of the night are generally unsuitable for *dérives*.'

35
Ibid.

36
Walter Benjamin, *The Arcades Project* (trans. Howard Eiland and Kevin Mclaughlin), Cambridge, MA and London: The Belknap Press, 1999, pp.427 and 453.

37
Charles Baudelaire, 'The Painter of Modern Life', *The Painter of Modern Life and Other Essays* (trans. Jonathan Mayne), London: Phaidon Press, 1995, p.9. Thirty years before this landmark essay was published, and more than a century before Debord conceived of his own 'theory of the *dérive*', Honoré de Balzac published a 'theory of walking' (originally titled *Théorie de la démarche*) as early as 1833, as part of his sprawling *Comédie humaine*. Like Baudelaire and Debord after him, Balzac clearly framed his interest in the culture of pedestrianism in the larger context of a decidedly *urban* anthropology. A very different literary reference is that of Robert Walser's 'The Walk' (1917), one of the most widely read short stories by the maverick modernist master of the miniature. *Flânerie* and *dérive* are at the heart, finally, of Leo Charney's very Walserian *Empty Moments: Cinema, Modernity, and Drift*, Durham: Duke University Press, 1998.

38
Fried was a tireless advocate of the work of Anthony Caro, who, as a leading figure at St. Martin's School of Art, was an important force in steering Long away from the established traditions of modern sculpture which he so authoritatively embodied. Long's decision, inspired by seeing Noguchi's work, to migrate his sculpture to the floor, was part of a historical thrust towards the creation of *situations*, which Fried denounced as experiential theatre rather than 'real' art. See Michael Fried, 'Art and Objecthood', originally published in *Artforum*, June 1967, pp.12—23, reprinted in *Art and Objecthood: Essays and Reviews*, Chicago: University of Chicago Press, 1998, pp.148—72; Mel Bochner, 'The Serial Attitude', *Artforum*, December 1967, pp.28—33; Sol LeWitt, 'Paragraphs on Conceptual Art', originally published in *Artforum*, June 1967, p.80, reprinted in Charles Harrison and Paul Wood (ed.), *Art in Theory: An Anthology of Changing Ideas 1900—2000*, Oxford: Wiley-Blackwell, 2002, p.846.

39
Silent Spring dealt with the disastrous effects of the boundless use of DDT and similar pesticides upon the natural environment, and *The Limits to Growth* with the rapid increase in the world's population and its impact on our natural environment (among many other things). See Rachel Carson, *Silent Spring*, Boston: Houghton Mifflin, 1962; and Donella H. Meadows, Dennis L. Meadows, Jorgen Randers and William W. Behrens III, *The Limits to Growth*, New York: Universe Books, 1972.

40
The success of the first Earth Day led to the founding of Greenpeace in Vancouver the following year. Other important dates and events surrounding the environmental turn in politics and society at large are the mass-scale dissemination in 1968 and 1972 of a series of iconic photographs made by NASA astronauts of the Earth seen from outer space; the first oil and energy crisis of 1973; and the publication in 1973 of Ernst Friedrich Schumacher's *Small Is Beautiful* treatise — 'a study of economics as if people mattered', according to its tagline. A decade and a half or so later,

even the effects of the Chernobyl nuclear disaster of 1986 indirectly filtered through into Long's practice, as remembered in the following anecdote by Hamish Fulton: 'Feng-shui (wind and water) Chernobyl. Six months before 26 April 1986, Richard Long and I drank river water, flowing through the land of the Lapps.' R. Long, *Walking in Circles*, *op. cit.*, p.245.

41
See C. Harrison and P. Wood (ed.), *Art in Theory*, *op. cit.*, pp.849—93.

42
One particularly radical answer to Baldessari's question 'what is to be done?' was formulated in 1970 by Baldessari himself, when he initiated his *Cremation Project*, which required the burning of all the paintings he made between 1953 and 1966 — an extreme instance of the so-called 'aesthetic of disappearance', which we will be returning to shortly.

43
Henri Lefebvre, *Critique of Everyday Life: Volume 1* (trans. John Moore), London and New York: Verso, 1991, p.127.

44
Both quoted in L.R. Lippard, *Six Years*, *op. cit.*, pp.55 and 45.

45
See http://www.hamish-fulton.com (last accessed on 11 April 2009).

46
R. Solnit, *Wanderlust*, *op. cit.*, p.272. This idea of assimilation is obviously the most problematic aspect of Solnit's charge: is assimilation really part of Long's artistic ambition in traipsing, say, across the Nazca Desert?

47
Quoted in Malcolm Andrews, *Landscape and Western Art*, Oxford: Oxford University Press, 1999, p.215. Referring to the essentially *cultural* — i.e. human-made — quality of much of the so-called 'natural' beauty of the English landscape (as we know it from Long's photographs among other Environmental art sources), Andre uncovered a critical blind spot of which Richard Long quickly became all too aware. Long no longer walks in the idealised void of a landscape from which all human presence has been evacuated — and this is not only so because such landscapes have become increasingly difficult (if not wholly impossible) to find. In the aforementioned book, Andrews argues convincingly for a genealogy of 'landscape art' as a form that is essentially born from an iconography concerning depictions of solitude, with the oldest forays in such art dating back to Bellini's 'portraits' of Saint Jerome in the wilderness.

48
The better-known Giant of Cerne Abbas and Long Man of Wilmington, images of which (as circumstantial evidence of sorts) often appear in Land art anthologies, are in fact seventeenth- and eighteenth-century creations. Needless to say the inclusion of such images, or of photographs of Stonehenge, in such anthologies does not necessarily reduce these cultic objects to the status of artworks: they belong to the history of land art (lower case) as a more general phenomenon, rather than to the history of Land art (upper case) as a historical movement.

49
'Five, six, pick up sticks / Seven, eight, lay them straight' (1980), in Ben Tufnell (ed.), *Richard Long: Selected Statements and Interviews*, London: Haunch of Venison, 2007, p.16. In 'Words After the Fact' (1982), Long adds: 'A walk marks time with an accumulation of footsteps.' *Ibid.*, p.25. In an artist's statement published on the occasion of Long's solo exhibition at Abbot Hall Art Gallery in Kendal in 1985, we are reminded: 'A walk is a simple way to pass and order time.' *Ibid.*, p.29.

50
Ibid., p.16.

51
Gilles Deleuze, *Difference and Repetition* (trans. Paul Patton), New York: Columbia University Press, 1994, p.1. On p.70, see the following quote from David Hume's *A Treatise of Human Nature* (1748): 'Repetition changes nothing in the object repeated, but does change something in the mind which contemplates it.'

52
Michel Foucault, *The Order of Things*, New York: Vintage, 1970, p.387.

53
See John Cage's statement 'to whom it may concern: the white paintings came first; my silent piece came later', prefacing the composer's essay 'On Rauschenberg, Artist, and His Work', in John Cage, *Silence: Lectures and Writings*, Middletown: Wesleyan University Press, 1973, p.98.

54
Conversation with the artist, January 2009. Long has also commented: 'I never studied Zen, which is maybe a wonderful way to study Zen. I take it as a compliment and great fact of life about Zen and my work if people find similarities.' R. Long, *Walking in Circles*, *op. cit.*, p.92.

55
G. Deleuze, *Difference and Repetition*, *op. cit.*, p.3.

56
Ibid.

57
Ibid., p.2.

58
Ibid., p.5.

59
Freud's famous explanation of 'the compulsion to repeat' as a pathology which must be ascribed to the unconsciously repressed was triggered by his observations of 'normal' child's play — of a child staging, all by himself, 'the disappearance and return of the objects within his reach'. Sigmund Freud, 'Beyond the Pleasure Principle' (trans. James Strachey), *The Pelican Freud Library, Vol. 11: On Metapsychology, The Theory of Psychoanalysis*, Harmondsworth: Penguin Books, 1984, p.285.

60
I invoke the imagery of the mandala here because of their casual resemblance to some of the sand drawings made by Long in the 1960s and 70s (not as practical jokes, to be sure). They are comparable to works such as *Connemara Sculpture* from 1971 (a circular stone sculpture laid out on a desolate plot of land in the Irish district of Connemara), which reference the Western mystical tradition that produced the famed labyrinths in the cathedrals of Amiens and Chartres. Incidentally, in the 'Magiciens de la terre' exhibition organised in Centre Georges Pompidou and Grande Halle, Parc de la Villette, Paris in 1989, Long's giant mural *Red Earth Circle* overlooked an even bigger Australian aboriginal sand painting.

61
See L.R. Lippard, *Six Years*, *op. cit.*, pp.172 and 225.

62
Keith Arnatt interviewed for the BBC, 1979; quoted in Anna Lovatt, 'Earth', paper given at the Henry Moore Institute, 4 March 2009, available at http://www.henry-moore-fdn.co.uk/docs/anna_lovatt__earth_0.pdf (last accessed on 6 December 2009). The comparison between Arnatt and Long is an interesting one in that both artists made conscious but very different use of photography in their work, with Long in the end consistently sticking to an 'amateur' attachment to the medium that Arnatt later in life chose to leave behind to become a 'real' (i.e. 'professional') photographer.

63
R. Walser, 'The Walk', *op. cit.*, p.61.

64
In 2007, a similar project was organised in Berlin by Gregor Schneider. *7:00—8:30PM; 05.31.2007* consisted of nothing other than a long queue of people waiting to be let into the State Opera to see nothing — more precisely, nothing other than themselves queuing or forming a 'line made by queuing'.

65
See Tony Godfrey, *Conceptual Art*, London: Phaidon Press, 1998, p.175.

66
Guy Debord, *The Society of the Spectacle* (trans. Ken Knabb), New York: Zone Books, 1994, p.135.

67
See the online source http://www.mediaartnet.org/works/zen-for-film (last accessed on 14 December 2009).

68
The Lannis Museum of Normal Art opened its doors in New York's East Village in 1967, and was dedicated to honouring the critical spirit of Ad Reinhardt, whose own contribution to art theory has often been reduced to his famous quip that 'art is art; everything else is everything else'. One of Kozlov's better-known pieces, a telegram sent to the Museum of Modern Art in New York, constituted her contribution to the seminal 'Information' exhibition organised at MoMA in 1970: 'Particulars related to the information not contained herein constitute the form of this action.' Quoted in Max Kozloff, 'The Trouble With Art-as-Idea', *Artforum*,

vol.12, no.1, September 1972, pp.33—37, reprinted in Alexander Alberro and Blake Stimson (ed.), *Conceptual Art: A Critical Anthology*, Cambridge, MA and London: The MIT Press, 1999, p.272.

69
Charlotte Posenenske is an interesting case in point: after having been in some of the same important early exhibitions as Long (most notably 'Dies alles, Herzchen, wird einmal dir gehören', organised in 1967 by Dorothea Loehr at her gallery in Frankfurt am Main), she decided to withdraw from art-making altogether in 1968 to study sociology at the Universität Frankfurt am Main. Her farewell to the art world lamented that 'though art's formal development has progressed at an increasing tempo, its social function has regressed. Art is a product of temporary topicality, yet, the market is minute, and prestige and prices rise the less topical the supply is. It is painful for me to face the fact that art cannot contribute to the solution of urgent social problems.' Quoted in Burkhard Brunn (ed.), *Charlotte Posenenske* (exh. cat.), Frankfurt a.M.: Museum für Moderne Kunst, 1990, p.40.

70
The notion of 'spectral evidence' refers to Ulrich Baer, *Spectral Evidence: The Photography of Trauma*, Cambridge, MA and London: The MIT Press, 2005.

71
Jeff Wall, 'Marks of Indifference: Aspects of Photography in, or as, Conceptual Art', in Ann Goldstein and Anne Rorimer (ed.), *Reconsidering the Object of Art: 1965—1975* (exh. cat.), Los Angeles: The Museum of Contemporary Art, 1995, p.253. The title of Wall's essay in fact references a fragment from Theodor Adorno's *Aesthetic Theory* (originally published in the late 1960s, though showing no evidence as to the author's awareness of the contemporary art debate), in which Adorno muses over art's gradual, necessary 'passage' into anti-art — its mark of indifference is a mark of a certain type of disappearance.

72
Ibid.

73
Ibid., p.254.

74
Another photographic book work from 1967, *Royal Road Test*, highlights a supplementary quality which must have appealed to an artist like Long: Ruscha's interest in a nomadic aesthetic of everyday roaming, embodied by the unstable, mobile gaze of the artist driving a car through Southern California's desert of signage, glass and concrete. Ruscha's influential book *Every Building on the Sunset Strip* (1964) is a line made by Los Angeles's favoured mode of transportation — driving. Ruscha's 'invention' of the modern artist's book came at a high historical price; in his 'Marks of Indifference' essay, Wall observes how 'Ruscha's books ruin the genre of "the book of photographs", that classical form in which art-photography declares its independence'. *Ibid.*, p.265. About *Twentysix Gasoline Stations* (1963), Wall says that 'only an idiot would take pictures of nothing but gas filling stations, and the existence of a book of just such pictures is a kind of proof of the existence of such a person'. *Ibid.*, p.266. These remarks resonate with previous observations regarding deadpan humour and the cultivation of a profound dumbness in so much early, conceptually driven post-Minimalist art practices.

75
Conversation with the artist, January 2009.

76
Curated by Willoughby Sharp upon the invitation of Thomas Leavitt, this groundbreaking exhibition also featured the work of Walter De Maria, Jan Dibbets, Hans Haacke, Michael Heizer, Neil Jenney, David Medalla, Robert Morris, Dennis Oppenheim, Robert Smithson and Gunther Uecker. The co-founder of *Avalanche* magazine, Sharp also devoted the journal's first issue, published in 1970, to the Earth art phenomenon. The first Land art exhibition in the US, titled 'Earth Works', was organised by Robert Smithson at Dwan Gallery in New York in 1968, and included Carl Andre, Herbert Bayer, De Maria, Heizer, Stephen Kaltenbach, Sol LeWitt, Morris, Claes Oldenburg, Oppenheim and Smithson himself.

77
J. Wall, 'Marks of Indifference', *op. cit.*, p.263.

78
Ibid., pp.264—65.

79
Ibid., p.263.

80
See Scott Watson, 'Urban Renewal: Ghost Traps, Collage, Condos, and Squats — Vancouver Art in the Sixties', in Dieter Roelstraete and Scott Watson (ed.), *Intertidal: Vancouver Art & Artists* (exh. cat.), Antwerp and Vancouver: MuHKA and Belkin Art Gallery, 2005, pp.31—44.

81
R. Walser, 'The Walk', *op. cit.*, p.63.

82
Elaine Scarry, *On Beauty and Being Just*, Princeton: Princeton University Press, 1999, p.51.